2/21/23

Richie –

Enjoy!

– Tom

Snapshots of My Father, John Silber

Snapshots of My Father, John Silber

Rachel Silber Devlin

Foreword by Lance Morrow

Peter E. Randall Publisher
Portsmouth, NH
2022

Published by
Peter E. Randall Publisher LLC
5 Greenleaf Woods Drive, Suite 102
Portsmouth, NH 03801

Cover photo of JRS by Ruth Silber
Book Design: Tim Holtz
Digital editing services provided by Allan Dines Photography

Printed in the United States of America

This book is dedicated with love
to my family
and all their abounding offspring.

Our first Boston University Commencement—and Pop's inauguration as president, in 1971. *Front row, left to right:* Kathryn, Laura Ruth, JRS, and David holding Caroline. *Back row:* Martha, Alexandra, Rachel, and Judith.
Boston University Photography.

"A sparrow would as eagle fly."

JOHN R. SILBER, 1946

Contents

Foreword

I THOUGHT OF ERNEST HEMINGWAY'S LINE "THE MOST COMPLI-cated subject that I know...is a man's life."

Was it true of John Silber? Was he a complicated character?

His life was active and complex—now and then, tumultuous. I grant that he seemed a paradox: a brilliant intellect with a talent for knocking heads; a philosopher who spent most of his professional life as a gladiator. He sliced through Gordian knots; he offended those who didn't like the way he used the blade.

But in my reading, the man himself was essentially simple—fiercely and even elegantly simple. I think he was too intelligent to be compli-cated. As Rachel Silber Devlin says in her lovely memoir, people either loved him or hated him. I am in the first category.

John could not have survived and succeeded as he did without his energy, will, and clarity of mind. He was penetratingly intelligent, quick, funny, coarse sometimes, ruthlessly candid, and now and then obnoxious and overbearing. He was always entirely *present*. This *direct-ness* struck me the first time I met him, at a tinkling and chattering cocktail party on Bay State Road. I never knew anyone quite so authen-tic or so present in the world—aware and available (aggressively avail-able, one might say) and as may be, ready for battle. He said what he thought. I never liked his moods of mockery, for they were not subtle, and they could wound; they were the downside of his honesty. He was not without cruelty. When he removed his armor, he was a very sweet man. He could be hilarious. He had eight children and a splendidly lively and devoted wife, Kathryn, and he loved them as intensely as he loved the university that he more or less created.

Those of us who were his partisans considered John a samurai genius—a knight-errant pledged to the defense of reason and sanity and his school. He was unafraid—a rare quality in university life. He had his head screwed on straighter and tighter than anyone else in the

xii   SNAPSHOTS OF MY FATHER

academic world, which was in the early stages of going to the dogs of ideology—though not, in his time, at Boston University.

He came up to Boston from Texas, and he played the Texan sometimes, a useful thing in the Hub of the Universe, especially among the professors. He liked to disconcert their solemnities. Everyone knows that Texans are apt to become a little more so when they travel east. It's a sort of vaudeville, which the performer enjoys as much as his audience does.

I was there one day, for example, when John summoned his University Professors to lunch in order to read them the riot act—in the Texas way.

In the University Professors program that he invented—a sort of elite college within the greater Boston University—John over the years assembled a distinguished faculty, including four Nobel Prize winners (Elie Wiesel, Saul Bellow, Derek Walcott, and the physicist Sheldon Glashow). John himself was a University Professor. There were about thirty others in various fields: classics, anthropology, history, literature, philosophy, economics, biology, and so on. I—a journalist without an advanced degree—may have been the least of the bunch. (After John left, the University Professors program was abolished).

It was rare—unheard of—for us all to have lunch together. I think the Nobel Prize winners were absent on this particular day; that was in part the issue that John wished to discuss. We gathered in a private room of the student union, nothing fancy—actually, just an alcove off to the side, away from the student traffic. John chose the site in order to dramatize the grievance he wanted to discuss: We were too big for our britches, we were lazy, we didn't show up enough, and we were costing him too goddamned much money.

We sat down to soggy vegetables. I chatted gloomily with my colleague Geoffrey Hill, the English poet. Harold Bloom claimed Geoffrey was the best poet then working in the language. In a few years, the Queen would bestow a knighthood upon him. Of Geoffrey's work, it was said, "His dominant mode was elegy." It was certainly the dominant mode of his conversation.

John joined us. He was a relatively small but straight-backed, handsome man with strong, square features (strong nose, jaw—one might even say strong hair, which was thick and wavy and vital.) His eye-glasses in dark plastic frames aged him a little, the lenses smudging and damping the fire in his eyes. His voice was an interesting instru-ment—flat and emphatic, with traces of his native San Antonio and thereabouts, but with (as one discovered) great fluency and endless intellectual resources that he had acquired over the years. I doubt that John ever forgot anything.

One of his charming qualities—for he had great charm at his dis-posal—was a capacity to surprise. His enemies (of whom there were many, especially among the professors at his own university) thought him a monster and a political reactionary, which was nonsense—evi-dence of their inattention. At the University of Texas, where he was Dean of Arts and Sciences before being fired in a policy dispute, he was a firm and principled liberal—a crusader against capital punishment and one of the authors of the nationwide Head Start program. Rachel explains his politics: "As he saw it, a liberal looks at all sides of an issue and listens to all voices."

But in his early days at Boston University, he had played rough and had been ruthless in cutting away the dead wood. The faculty revolted and signed petitions that demanded he be dismissed. The board demurred. He outplayed his enemies; by the time I got there in the mid-1990s, the mediocre and faltering institution that he took over in 1971 was a leading, prospering research university with a bal-anced budget. The university's net worth had increased almost 1,200 percent.

Assembled for lunch, we University Professors talked quietly and uneasily among ourselves (*what is this all about?*). At length, John tapped a water glass with his spoon and, summoning up the full San Antonio, embarked upon his speech to the University Professors:

"I hate to piss in your punchbowl," he began, employing a flat, gun-slinger's voice. There was a touch of Tom Dunson in it—the autocratic John Wayne trail boss in the movie *Red River*.

On this occasion, John relied upon artfully applied boorishness. It worked to get people's attention and focus their minds, although of course he paid a price for it in the grumblings and discontent of the faculty lounges.

o   o   o

One can overdo the Texas thing when discussing John Silber. It's too easy. It has elements of caricature. John was after all a world-class intellectual himself and a considerable connoisseur of intellectual talent in many fields. That's how he assembled such an impressive faculty. Still, the John Wayne side of his style was bracing when considered in contrast to the ways of the academic departments—the petty and joyless intrigues, which were so vicious sometimes that one thought of the empress dowager's eunuchs scheming in the Forbidden City.

Harry Truman—whom John resembled in a couple of ways (fearlessness, a habit of speaking plainly)—used to keep a set of Plutarch's *Parallel Lives* at hand. He claimed that in Plutarch, he could find pretty much everything he needed to know about men's behavior, especially that of leaders. (He was speaking in an earlier age, before one said *men and women*.)

I would like to have seen a profile of John Silber written by Plutarch, who would have captured John's ambitions, his intense moral and political reasoning, his incisive mind. Once, John was talking to his driver about the Stephen Hawking book called *A Brief History of Time*. The driver, named Richie, mentioned the Big Bang as the beginning of the universe. John came back with a Socratic query: "What banged?" Ah.

Plutarch would have talked (as Rachel does) about John's birth-flaw—the right arm that ended in a stub where the elbow would have been. Was John's character to be explained by that circumstance—one that he scorned to conceal? People wondered whether his occasional ferocity was a defense to ward off anything as insulting as pity.

Plutarch, in a well-known passage, wrote: "...the most glorious exploits do not always furnish us with the clearest discoveries of virtue or vice in men; sometimes a matter of less moment, an expression or a jest, informs us better of their character and inclinations, than the most famous sieges, the greatest armaments...."

Rachel Silber Devlin's fine portrait of her father is filled with such illuminating private detail, with stories that would have been unavailable to anyone who had not been there for all of those years—anyone who was not John Silber's child. Her rendering has a transcendent objectivity and clarity and understanding that could only come from having known him as she did. Here are the Texas roots, the antecedents—the cultural and family background, the accumulation of intimate and accidental details, the stories.

It was telling that John gave his grandchildren sets of the McGuffey Readers, the nineteenth-century primers that arguably did more to form the American character than all the works of Hawthorne, Poe, Melville, and Whitman. At least 120 million copies of the McGuffeys were sold between 1836 and 1920—sales that rivaled those of the Bible and *Webster's Dictionary*. William McGuffey, the author, was, like John, a philosopher and college president. Along with grammar, McGuffey taught promptness, kindness, honesty, and telling the truth.

Such lessons, John thought, represented a good start.

LANCE MORROW

Preface

M̲Y̲ ̲M̲O̲T̲H̲E̲R̲ ̲W̲O̲U̲L̲D̲ ̲B̲E̲ ̲H̲O̲R̲R̲I̲F̲I̲E̲D̲ ̲B̲Y̲ ̲T̲H̲I̲S̲ ̲B̲O̲O̲K̲. D̲I̲D̲ I̲ ̲N̲O̲T̲ ̲L̲E̲A̲R̲N̲ anything from her example? She would see telling our family's stories as akin to undressing in front of a picture window and parading back and forth, making a spectacle of myself. There could be no good reason for doing so. I did consider fictionalizing the whole thing. Mother could have enthusiastically gotten behind such a project. She loved the Nancy Mitford novels in which Mitford portrayed her father as Uncle Matthew, cracking his whip on the front lawn and grinding his dentures to bits in his fury.

My dad didn't have an inordinate sense of privacy, but I think he would try to talk me down from the cliff over some parts of this book. He often let fly with incredibly honest and bluntly candid comments, and he wasn't terribly secretive or self-protective about much of his private life, but that doesn't mean he would like one of his children to tell too much. You see, he always felt *he* was the one to brandish his own views, and he expected us children to be more circumspect.

So why do it? The answer is simple: I couldn't help myself. Once I started reminiscing on paper, it all came tumbling out. I also felt I was circling and circling my father, trying with each layer to approach an accurate impression of him. In the early chapters, the Background, I go into the family influences in his formative years, without which the layers of meaning that motivated his life would be missing. In the middle chapters, the Foreground, I look at my mother, my siblings and me, and Pop's trajectory from Texas to Boston University and what life was like there, including his run for governor of Massachusetts. In the final chapters, the Patina, I describe the later years, the hardships he weathered, and his continued accomplishments while out of the public eye. As works of art take on an extra richness as they age, so did Pop's character take on a mantle of valor and validity as he was severely tested by debility and fate.

Each chapter, besides fitting into the larger narrative, can stand alone. If you wish, you can jump ahead to the chapters that interest you most, but I hope you will then go back and read this book in its entirety to take in the full picture.

Ultimately, it is important that I tell the story because I'm one of the few who knows it and because John Silber, the man, is so widely misunderstood. People who knew him either love him or hate him. None are indifferent.

This book, a memoir, is in no way a full biography of my dad's life. That would require several volumes plus a lifetime of study, and this was not a research project. As the title implies, each chapter is like a snapshot taken from my perspective, peering into the past I saw.

Nevertheless, I do not believe these are merely superficial glimpses. As old photographs reveal details that become apparent when you gaze at them and study them, working on each chapter brought forward long-forgotten details and pointers. There are gaps in the narrative and people important to Pop who don't appear on these pages. Like pulling photos out of a box, there is some randomness involved. At any rate, I would inevitably, and necessarily, be leaving something out. His vast interests and experience would be impossible to incorporate into one book. My siblings have "snapshots" of their own that I hope they will record in books or works of art. Our combined efforts would create a more complete picture, a fine mosaic.

When we were very young, we all called our parents Mama and Daddy. Then, at a certain age, while trying to sound more grown up, I switched to saying Mother rather than Mama. Around the same time, I realized that too often there was a whine in my voice when I said Daddy. As in, "Oh Daddy, why can't I go?" I started calling our dad "Pop" then because, in its simplicity, that name does not lend itself to whining. I felt this was a step toward maturity and independence, but I still reverted to Daddy at times and archly addressed him as Father on occasion. Many of us, including his office staff, sometimes referred to him by his initials, JRS, and other family members have their own, mostly affectionate names for Pop.

My parents were sometimes exasperating, but always fascinating. They maintained a youthful mental vigor to the end, and they accomplished so much, taking my siblings and me along for the ride. Even as an adult, I remained close to these two attractive twin stars, never orbiting very far afield, always finding their part of the universe more vital. My children have often accused me of having a wonderful childhood, and I have to admit: Guilty as charged.

PART ONE

Background

Forces that Marked the Man

1

Mammy

My father was the only one who called Grandma "Mammy." And it wasn't *his* mother either. She was my mother's mother, his mother-in-law, so often a dread figure in men's lives. But he didn't call her Mammy sarcastically or as a joke, although he probably got the name from Mammy Yokum, a character he loved in the Al Capp comic strip. It was always an expression of fondness, a claiming of a special, sympathetic, and friendly relationship with his wife's mother.

Mammy was what you would call a handsome woman. She was tall, broad-shouldered, and impressive. Her face and frame looked quite a bit like the Statue of Liberty. It came as no surprise and seemed quite fitting to me when I learned that the model for the Statue of Liberty had been the French sculptor's mother-in-law. At rest, her face showed some of the ravages of the Great Depression in her rather skeptical, dark eyes and the dour set of her lips. However, her great heart exploded forth from her entire being when she was animated.

For me, it was the fervor of her affection that made me love her. No one else hugged me so tight or kissed me so emphatically or was willing to swing me as long as I liked, all the while talking and singing to me. Yet for Pop, I think it was mostly her strength and her indomitable way of creating a beautiful life in the face of a dirt-poor background. The house my mother grew up in did not have indoor plumbing or electricity until sometime in her teens. They used kerosene lamps and listened to a battery-operated radio. My mother's dad played the violin, and Mammy seemed to make meals out of nothing: biscuits from scratch; tomatoes, beans, and Swiss chard from the garden; agarita jelly from the bushes that grew wild not far from the house.

More recently, she would take a bucket of the smallest fish you ever saw, caught by my son, John, and she cleaned and breaded those fish and fried them up for a tasty feast. What my father told me he admired so much about my mother's family was the fact that even though they had much less wherewithal than his family, they did not let that stop them from going where they wanted and doing what they wanted.

When they wished to travel to the coast or to another state, they would pile into the car with food Mammy had prepared and water that they would take along and bedrolls that they could sleep on when they camped out. My grandpa would strap canisters of gasoline to the outside of the car. (I don't remember exactly what I was told about how Grandpa got hold of this gasoline, but somehow he skimmed it or acquired it from wells or refineries where he sometimes worked.)

Pop was a bit envious and impressed that they had traveled so much during the Depression. Because they were able to rough it, they didn't need to stay in hotels or go to restaurants all the time. They probably did look like hicks with everything strapped onto the outside of their car, but they happily stretched their horizons because they were not too full of themselves to appear so.

My dad followed this model during all of my growing-up years. When we traveled with a car full of kids, as many as seven by the time my parents were done, we always brought along air mattresses and pumps that were worked by pressing down on them repeatedly with a foot. That way we never needed more than one hotel room.

Pop always liked to get an early start on the road, and some of my fondest memories are of taking off before dawn and riding along in the dark, drinking delicious coffee from a thermos cup. We also made sandwiches or bought rotisserie chickens to eat for lunches in the car or on the side of the road, and Pop had a little table with tripod legs that he put together as a serving station for these roadside meals. In this fashion, my parents somehow took their ever-growing family across the country repeatedly and even traveled all around Europe several times. Just think about it, this was before the advent of paper diapers.

Pop also admired Mammy because she was a shrewd business-woman. All her life she had listened to oilmen talk about where the oil was found. She listened very well and she kept a map of her own, marking where the existing, profitable oil wells were. Then, during the Depression, she and Grandpa barely scraped together the cash to buy a small piece of land that her map promised would produce.

The resulting well that she owned a share in didn't make her rich, but it paid off the investment several times over and provided her with a subsidiary income for most of her life. She still lived quite frugally, but she was always very generous to her children and grandchildren.

During World War II, she worked at Kelly Field in San Antonio, charged with getting aircraft repaired and flying again. Even later, and on through the Vietnam War, she continued in the same job. She also liked to study the stock market, although she invested very little in it. In the early morning, over coffee, she would study her *Standard and Poor's* along with her *Farmer's Almanac*.

I sometimes wonder what it was like when my mother brought Pop home to meet her parents. At first they probably were none too keen on this young man with only one hand. There was also the fact that his father was a German immigrant. Mammy's sister, Aunt Kate (pronounced "Ain't Kate"), once referred to my dad disparagingly as "pure D German." I knew she meant he was very German, and it wasn't a compliment. At the time I thought the "D" was for Deutsch because I knew that meant German, but later I learned that some Texans called things "pure D" when they meant they were very much of something. Some said the "D" was for damn.

Aunt Kate's husband was a Texan of German descent, so she had her own personal idea of what a trial Germans could be. Also, with the war against Germany just ending, that could not have been a quality that recommended my dad to them, and if they had known, as Pop would later discover, that his German heritage was, in fact, Jewish, it is doubtful that this would have mitigated matters.

There was also probably some anti-intellectual sentiment involved in Aunt Kate's pronouncement. My dad liked to tell a joke that underscored how striving to become educated gained very little respect in some quarters. As he would tell it: With all the family and friends gathered when a young man came home from college, his father asked him to tell them something he had learned. So, the young man said proudly, "Pi r squared." His father then grimaced, shook his head sadly, and said quietly, "No son, pies are round. Cornbread are square."

Although my violin-playing grandpa adored his daughter, Kathryn, from the moment she was born and for the rest of his life, truth be told, my mother was not the kind of daughter Mammy would have chosen for herself. She was always trying to "pretty up" little Kathryn and push her to make more of herself. She dressed her daughter in dresses made from flour sacks and curled her hair with a scalding curling iron. She also sent Kathryn to a neighbor who taught elocution and public speaking classes, but despite these efforts, my mother always retained an innate elegance and natural reticence that resisted becoming the outgoing type Mammy wished for. All the while, all little Kathryn really wanted to do was read and listen to musical programs on the radio with her dad.

By the time Pop came calling, an intellectual and artist from a relatively refined family, Kathryn had made it clear that her own goals for herself were fairly highbrow and she had quite left her mystified mother in the dust with her prodigious study of esoteric subjects. At the age of fifteen, the summer before she began college at Trinity University in San Antonio, my mother took the bus to the college several days a week in order to teach Greek to a few professors. She had taught the language to herself.

Mammy could probably see that this bright young man, her daughter's debate partner, was a pretty good match for her. Also, this suitor had a way of pleasing Mammy because he gave her respect and expressed an interest in her thinking. My grandpa, who was a humorist along the lines of Will Rogers, gave his imprimatur, saying of the boyish Johnny, "That young fellow is going to make a good living all his life without ever picking up anything heavier than a pencil."

2

Jewell

WE CALLED MY DAD'S MOTHER "GRANDMOTHER" UNTIL SHE HAD her first great-grandchild and renamed herself "Granny-Great." We grandchildren liked the name so much that many of us started calling her Granny-Great as well. This caused a terrible fury in her longtime rival, Mammy. "Well, from now on I'll be Great-Great-Grandma-Great!" she proclaimed. But that didn't catch on.

Texas women are a tough breed. Perhaps it is something about the ranching background that produces this tenacity. A ranch woman had to be able to give orders to a bunkhouse full of cowboys in a way that commanded their respect, rather than asking for it. If you have to ask for respect, and wait around hoping others will confer it on you, you might as well give up. On the iconic television series, *Dallas*, when Bobby Ewing was begging his daddy to give him the power, old Jock put it so succinctly: "Power isn't something you give; it's something you take." The women on both sides of my family tree didn't wait around to be empowered; they were always forces to be reckoned with.

While both my grandmothers were strong women, they had very different styles. Mammy was rough and ready, while my dad's mother, named Jewell, was distinctively feminine, the last of the Southern belles. I can see her in my mind's eye, barely taller than five feet; she never went outside into the Texas sunshine without her long white gloves, an elegant sun hat, and her parasol unfurled. Jewell was invariably well-coiffed and elaborately appointed. Her carefully styled outfits were always just so, tailored to perfection, and she always wore jewelry—how could she not with her name.

Jewell had been quite a beauty in her youth and she maintained a glamorous attitude all her life. I used to watch her looking in the mirror, even in her seventies and eighties, as she touched the back of her hair with a well-manicured hand, and I felt that what she saw in the glass was nothing short of Lana Turner in her heyday. This was the sort of glamorous existence that Jewell envisioned for herself.

Grandmother Jewell also had a definite idea about how she wanted to present her two sons, Paul Jr. and Johnny, to the world. When they were very young she dressed them in little suits, and she let my father's hair grow into long blond curls. She must have gotten the idea from the popular book *Little Lord Fauntleroy*. Pop's older brother did him the favor of cutting his hair short when he was about three. As Pop recalled, he was relieved to finally "look like a boy." Nonetheless, my sisters and I always love to look at the early pictures of our dad with charming curls cascading over his boyish shoulders. In most family pictures, as the boys grew up, Paul and John are dressed smartly in suits or well-ironed shirts and trousers, and a bit later Paul would be wearing his military uniform.

However, it was not always easy for Jewell to maintain this elegant presence. When she married my grandfather, he was a well-to-do architect. As a wedding present, he gave her a little coupe that she loved to drive, and they lived in a large house with servants. However, as the Great Depression undermined their prosperity, Granddaddy could not find work, and they had to move to a much smaller abode. These were impecunious times, and my dad could recall mending the roof using tin cans by taking off the lid and bottom, cutting down the length, and spreading the tin flat so it could be slipped under a leaking shingle.

In the face of these hardships, Jewell didn't just sit and despair; she went back to teaching and was able to support the family. Before her marriage, she had taught for about ten years in a one-room schoolhouse. While out of work, Granddaddy helped with the cooking and, perhaps from spending so much time in the kitchen, came up with the idea for a corn chip that he called Masa Crisp. These were tortilla chips with lemon and sugar sprinkled over them. During my childhood, whenever we went to a Mexican restaurant, Pop would sprinkle lemon juice and sugar over a fresh hot tortilla so we could taste it and imagine what Masa Crisps were like.

Granddaddy went to California with his idea, trying to get the backing to start production, but Jewell refused to budge, and she was still there, in San Antonio, sustaining the family when he came back, having failed in his purpose. I once asked Pop if he didn't think it was rather hard of his mother, refusing to go along and take the family to California where she could have helped Granddaddy realize his dream. But he felt she had done the right thing, keeping the family going. If she hadn't held firm, they might have lost everything.

Grandmother Jewell could also be quite funny. When playing canasta, she would pretend to straighten up the discard deck while taking a peek at what had been played. It was very obvious that she was doing this and we would laugh and mimic her. She didn't mind, as she had gotten the information she wanted. Once, when we were having tea, she told us about how, when they were poor, they served "tea" with just a pot of boiling water that they poured into china cups with cream and sugar, in essence, having a tea party with no tea.

Moreover, she would regale us with stories of her childhood, living at her grandmother's house in Cameron, Texas. One time, she and her cousin had resented having to churn the milk, so they spit into the churn and laughed themselves silly when anyone ate some of the resulting butter. She also described drying part of a bumper crop of those beautiful Texas freestone peaches by laying them out in halves on a clean white sheet draped over the flat roof of a shed. All her life she was very nostalgic about her upbringing. Whenever she tried out a new pen, she wrote the name of the town where she grew up: Cameron.

What Cameron signified for her was an idyllic Victorian world, an orderly existence regulated by old-world virtues. She tried to re-create this golden atmosphere in her home. I remember a thought-ful order, with handmade lace coverings over the arms of plush chairs and couches. She would sometimes play the old melodeon in the living room. It looked like a low, upright piano, but by gently pumping the pedals with her feet it produced organ music. The beds were always made when not in use, and each had a neat, quilted satin cover. Every-where you looked the house was clean, comfortable, and welcoming. The only obvious note of modernity, the telephone, was relegated to a nook in the hall.

Besides being decorous and amusing, Jewell could suddenly deliver a veiled insult without notice. As my late husband, Jim, remarked after one of her insinuating comments, "Your grandmother does serve a spicy cider." As a girl, I had my back up, always prepared to defend my mother or Mammy against the snide rejoinders Grandmother Jewell was likely to drop. One Thanksgiving, when we were loading the silverware into the dishwasher, she remarked in her Texas drawl to no one in particular, "I always wash my good silver by hand." The implication of many of her asides being that my mother's housekeeping was in some way subpar.

Furthermore, Pop was usually oblivious to these undercurrents and once he even seemed to support his mother's point of view. When we were preparing to spend a year in London, I felt Pop insulted my mother when he asked Grandmother Jewell to come help clean our house. The plan was that for the first few months, before we found a place of our own in London, we would be switching houses with the internationally well-regarded philosopher, John N. Findlay, and his family. Pop wanted our house to be spic and span, hence the call to his mother. I felt this move as an affront to my mother's status, but she never seemed to mind any of it. And looking back, I wonder who got the better of whom? There was Jewell, with a dishtowel turbaned around her red curls, cleaning away with my siblings and me as her minions while my mother was free to concentrate on packing.

Jewell also had a penchant for lying about her age when she was forced to reveal it. She even lied about it on her driver's license. Pop said she didn't fib by much on the license, only a couple of years, which seemed pretty comical to me since she was about sixty-five at the time. For her birthday one year, Pop took a long sheet of white craft paper and drew on it a life-sized and very true-to-life picture of Grandmother Jewell wearing her sun hat and a polka dot dress. He colored in the portrait and filled in each polka dot with a number. At her birthday party, attended by the whole family, including my dad's brother, Uncle Paul, and his family, we played "Pin the Age on Grandmother." I remember, when it was Uncle Paul's turn, he pinned her age at 180.

She was none too pleased by this fun. She had a way of emitting a ripple of negative energy created by some metamorphosis of incensed thought being compressed by her brain. This invariably cast a pall on those present. At any rate, on this occasion, Pop let her off the hook in the end, when at the culmination of the game, he brought forth a sealed envelope containing a document that read: *This is to certify that Grandmother Jewell Silber is sixteen years old.*

Once when Jewell was visiting us, we heard that a childhood friend of ours had been ordained a minister in the Lutheran Church. I asked Grandmother Jewell what she thought of that, as some people would not approve of a female minister. She surprised us all by saying, "I don't see anything wrong with a woman becoming a minister." Then she paused, before adding, "I wouldn't worship in her church," as her voice trailed off thoughtfully.

In her nineties, Grandmother Jewell lived with my parents for a while. During this sojourn, Pop introduced her to the tangerine liqueur, Mandarine Napoléon. After a lifetime of teetotal existence, the charm of this libation was a surprise to her. She looked forward to it, always served in a dainty antique glass in the evening when he came home from the office. Pop also sometimes secretly mixed a little into her Ensure so she would drink it.

One quality my dad shared with his mother was a sort of deliberation in his movements. In Grandmother Jewell, it came across as being unhurried. I never saw her run or speed up her actions in any way. She invariably moved and worked at a slow, steady pace. Contrastingly, Pop did rush, and he was usually on a tight, super-packed schedule. He was also very light on his feet and would often spontaneously dance around a room or along a sidewalk, but if you looked closely, there was always a deliberation in his actions that reminded me of her. And when he was relaxing, puttering around in his study or garage, or working with clay on a sculpture, his slow movements directed by thought and intent were very recognizably similar to his mother's.

When Jewell died, at the age of ninety-eight, she didn't forget about her appearance. She had made all the arrangements and even chosen her outfit, a seafoam-green evening gown with matching shoes, and her longtime, aged hairdresser attended to her coiffure and makeup.

3

Paul G.

Pop loved his father, in a tender, protective way. He fondly remembered the things he said or did and never faulted him. Grandmother Jewell always referred to her late husband as "Paul G." The "G" was for Georg, anglicized to George. Paul G. was German, and whenever my dad quoted his father he would put on a thick German accent. I only remember my grandfather as an elegant, mustached presence, always with a cigar and smiling eyes. My older brother, David, remembered visiting our grandparents and rubbing candles on the driveway with his cousin, Paulette, so that Granddaddy's car would skid. His impression was that she thought he was mean, but he didn't know why.

Our dad seemed proud of his father when he described the rather severe methods of his child rearing. Pop would sometimes describe how his father had maintained discipline or taught his brother, Paul, and him lessons when we kids complained to him about his own treatment of us, such as the way he was relentlessly intent on our maintaining good posture. His usual command when he saw one of us slouching was that we should "pop that sternum!" The theory being that if you held your chest forward with pride, everything else fell into place. Our dad told us that his father used to make him and his brother hold cut-off broomsticks behind their backs with their arms bent back over the rod and tied to it, forcing them to retain perfect posture for long periods of time. This sounded like torture to us, but he said that it seemed to work. I must admit, Johnny and Paul Jr. always did hold their shoulders back admirably even into advanced age.

Johnny continued to live with his parents when he went to college at Trinity University near his home in San Antonio. Yet he managed to fully participate in campus life, joining the debate team and becoming one of the founding members and first president of a fraternity, the Triniteers. During this time, his father presented him with a "contract of the house." It listed the hours he would maintain, the chores he would be responsible for, and stipulated that he would stay away from alcohol. If he wanted to live at home, he had to sign the contract. I asked Pop if he found that to be a bit strict. He said that of course he did, but that he approved of the tactic as a great incentive for a young person to become independent.

Johnny first learned to draw and sculpt from his father. Paul G. was an architect, but also a sculptor. Often, his buildings had decorative, sculpted elements. Sadly, many are now gone. The cast stone façade of the YMCA building that was formerly next to the Texas Theatre on the main drag in Austin, across from the university, had beautifully sculpted decorative elements done by my grandfather. David pointed it out to me once when we went to a dance there as teenagers. The YMCA is now gone, replaced by a large, sterile Church of Scientology building.

My grandmother, Jewell, often took her grandchildren, when they visited her individually, to have lunch in a restaurant called the Camellia Room, located in the old Joske's department store near the Alamo in downtown San Antonio. The room and its decorations were designed by my grandfather and looked like the set for a movie starring Fred Astaire and Ginger Rogers. It was a broad space, with elegant banquettes; you could imagine Fred and Ginger sweeping in and exchanging clever repartee over glasses of champagne. I'm sure my grandmother liked to go there to reminisce about romantic experiences of her own. The lamps Granddaddy designed, real works of art, were patterned after camellia flowers. The building has since been gutted and is now part of a shopping mall with what the promotional brochure calls "many fast-casual restaurants."

There may be numerous other buildings with decorative sculptures that Granddaddy designed and created still in existence across Texas. I wish we had asked my dad and his brother, Paul, to record the ones they recalled so that we could go and see them. The only extant example I know of for sure is the decoration around the steeple of the chapel at the University of the Incarnate Word in San Antonio. Granddaddy sculpted the large, white, trumpeting angels that face four directions around the steeple. They are very beautiful and unusual, and their size makes them an imposing spectacle as their winged, white forms, trumpets raised, stand out against the red brick of the steeple and the blue of the sky.

The modest house my grandparents lived in, and that Jewell continued to live in after her husband's death, had features designed by Paul G. A bathroom Granddaddy added onto the back of the house had an extra-large, beautifully tiled, walk-in shower. Across the lawn at the edge of the property, he built a patio with a small kitchen area that was a marvelous space for festive get-togethers or relaxing solitude. The floor was made of beautiful ceramic tile. My dad remembered driving down to Mexico with his dad to find the tile. This outdoor living area was always cool and shaded because Granddaddy built his study above it.

Young Johnny acted as an apprentice to his father, traveling around Texas with him to work on the buildings Paul G. had designed. That was where my dad began to learn about architecture and everything involved in building. When I was six, our family moved into a large red brick house near the university in Austin. Pop was involved in every aspect of the renovations there. The masterpiece was his study, built over the garage, with a high-pitched roof to accommodate extra-tall, built-in bookcases. He added a walkway from the study to the second floor of the main house, so he could go back and forth with ease. Pop also had the large closets on the third floor lined with cedar to keep moths away, and he had a water faucet installed in a small closet in the wall across from the top of the third-floor stairs. There was always a coiled hose there, attached to the faucet, ready to go in case of fire.

In keeping with the beautiful design of the old house, he had the brick walkways along the front extended all the way around it, making a charming path to walk. He also commissioned a large round table, especially designed to just fit into the back screened porch by the kitchen where we ate in warm weather. Its notable feature was a sizable lazy Susan at the center, facilitating the passing of dishes for our large family. Later, when we came to Boston, Pop was interested and engaged in every detail of improvements to the campus.

When we first arrived, he had elaborate plans for covering over the Mass Pike that runs beside the university to gain more space and create a beautiful grassy campus. This evidently was too grand a scheme and impossible to realize. His proposal to enhance the campus in the opposite direction, covering over Storrow Drive and extending the "BU Beach" to the edge of the Charles River got a bit further. Architects and engineers outlined the project and created impressive drawings, but this plan eventually fell through as well.

His sharp eye and experience added considerably to the design of the many large and handsome buildings that were constructed during his tenure. JRS loved the old brick townhouses on Bay State Road, and the university bought them up over the years.

Pop was always thinking of ways to improve the grounds and make them more beautiful. When he and my mother accompanied me and my very young children to Disneyland, he seemed less interested in the rides and more interested in questioning the maintenance crews about their methods to glean valuable tactics for Boston University.

After learning to sculpt from his dad, young John studied seriously with the sculptor Pompeo Coppini, the acclaimed artist who sculpted the Littlefield Fountain at the University of Texas among many other works. Whenever we children accompanied our dad to his office, we would always stop and look at the famous fountain of bronze horses with webbed hooves ridden by mermen beneath the boat of a winged Columbia, the female embodiment of the United States. My dad admired the sculptor's skill and also his manly personality.

A female student once wore red lipstick to class, and Coppini strode over to her and smeared it roughly across her face with his thumb. Pop told me this story when I was trying out makeup, my new look for junior high. He admired the way Coppini had insisted that a young woman should let the texture and structure of her face work their magic rather than coating it with color. Pop wasn't actually against lipstick, but he wanted me to know that it was unnecessary, and that there were times when it might not be appropriate, the classroom being one of them, where the focus should be on the work. He also just liked telling the story because he loved the way Coppini had ruled the domain of his studio with the force of his will and personality.

That's why I loved the story, too. I had read *Jane Eyre*, and Coppini seemed attractively domineering to me like a Mr. Rochester, but even better, a Mr. Rochester who was an artistic genius. With my father as an example, I couldn't imagine anything worse than a man with a weak spirit, and, of course, as a budding teenager, an image was beginning to form in my mind of what the object of my affection would be like.

My grandfather was once commissioned to sculpt a Brahman bull for a cattle association. He gave the job to young Johnny. My dad has admitted that he believed he was an even better sculptor than his father by that time. When the job was finished, Granddaddy signed his name to Johnny's statue, outraging Jewell, who thought their son should get credit for his own work. Paul G. maintained that it was the custom for an artist to sign any work that came from his studio. Pop seemed content with the way it all turned out. He was pleased with his mother for sticking up for him and was happy to let his father take credit for the work, having just a tincture of pity for "the old man" because he believed his dad could not have done quite as fine a job.

Paul G. was also a lifelong Boy Scout leader, a perfect calling for him because of his belief in doing things the right way. Like his wife, Jewell, he came from a Victorian background steeped in firm notions of honor and virtue, but Jewell's worldview was more fanciful and gentle than her husband's. The Bible verses that she read daily and the hymns she might sing spontaneously had a childlike simplicity and charm. The lessons she believed in were those of *The Secret Garden* by Frances Hodgson Burnett and books by others of her day, Victorians who wrote about learning to be kind, do good deeds, appreciate your surroundings, and cultivate nature to create a beautiful world. One of Jewell's favorite characters was Eppie, from George Eliot's *Silas Marner*, whose simplicity and goodness of heart epitomized the lessons of that age.

Paul G.'s Victorian framework was distinctly German, from the Black Forest and the old world of the beautiful, but cruel, fairy stories of the brothers Grimm. Pop introduced us to these tales by reading them to us in German the year we lived in Germany. He also read us the book of dark lessons for children, called *Der Struwwelpeter*. This book fascinated us with its pictures of a child who burns down the house when playing with matches and another child whose thumbs get chopped off because he won't stop sucking them. These examples give some understanding of the man who could have tied his sons' arms behind their backs in order to teach them to stand up straight.

The Victorian world of Paul G. and Jewell influenced in every way the upbringing of their sons. Pop felt those lessons and those of

Christianity informed every moral stand he would later take. He tried to give us, his kids, the benefit of that training by taking us to Sunday school each week, even though he no longer regularly attended church himself. Later, when we had children of our own, he bought us each sets of the McGuffey Readers, graded readers for teaching children to read that were originally used in the 1800s. The stories in them were repositories of the moral lessons our dad grew up with.

All of these lessons would have come to the fore in the leadership of Paul G. with his Boy Scouts. If Johnny and Paul were ever in his troop, it must not have been for very long. My dad told us stories about playing outrageous pranks on their hapless leader. They once peed in his car radiator and laughed like maniacs when it stank to high heaven on the way home from their campout. Paul and Johnny would never have tried something like that on their dad, who exuded rectitude and would find them morally odious if he heard of them doing such a thing.

The lady next door was an avid gardener, as was Paul G. They became good friends, discussing their plantings across the backyard fence. He affected a chivalrous attitude toward the lady, who incidentally had a husband. Granddaddy once remarked to Johnny that the lady's husband seemed quite passive and did not give her much of a hand around the house. To this his son piped up, spilling the gossip that his Uncle Bobby was helping out quite a lot over there and even sleeping with the woman. Pop could see immediately that his father was struck to the quick by the thought of his ne'er-do-well brother-in-law being on intimate terms with this woman that he honored. Young John scrambled to try to repair the damage he had done to the equilibrium of his father's universe. He said that he was just making it up because he thought it would be funny, and he let his father chew him out for inventing scandalous chatter about decent people.

Granddaddy's fortunes rose and fell and rose again during his lifetime. He first came to America in 1902, as a sculptor to help build the German Pavilion at the St. Louis World's Fair. He traveled in steerage, the least expensive and also least comfortable accommodation on an ocean liner, arriving with very little money. After establishing himself in Texas, where there was a large German community, he built his reputation and was well-to-do when he courted Jewell.

During the Depression, when the family moved to a much smaller house, he nevertheless refused to take work as a draftsman because he believed if he did so he would lose his professional standing and never be able to claim he was an architect again. Pop wasn't sure if this was true, but he admired his dad for sticking to his principles and realized it was also a matter of pride.

When Granddaddy's business was doing well again during the fifties, my dad tried to help him take the deductions he deserved on his income taxes, but Paul G. refused. He was so pleased and grateful to be making a good income, he wrote his check to the United States government with joy and signed it with a flourish.

4

Ma Bess

I only knew Mother Bessie as an elderly great-grandmother, but my impression of her as a merry Buddha is borne out even in early pictures. She was plump and smiling; her eyes actually seemed to invert into half-moons. She wore her hair in a small topknot on the crown of her head and her somewhat heavy lower jaw would hang slightly loose as she smiled. Johnny and his brother, Paul, called their grandmother Ma Bess, and she was known throughout the family and even to my mother's family as Mother Bessie, Ma Bessie, or Ma Bess.

My dad felt that she was the one person in the world who loved him with no reservations. When he was punished and sent to bed with no supper, she would bring him something to eat, and though she might not verbally sympathize, her affectionate, loving nature would comfort him. When Johnny had scarlet fever as a young child and was confined to his bed for many weeks, he did not suffer from pain so much as from boredom, and Ma Bess spent long hours with him, distracting him with conversation and reading to him. He remembered her reading "The Land of Counterpane" from *A Child's Garden of Verses*:

> When I was sick and lay a-bed,
> I had two pillows at my head,
> And all my toys beside me lay
> To keep me happy all the day.
>
> And sometimes for an hour or so
> I watched my leaden soldiers go,
> With different uniforms and drills,
> Among the bed-clothes, through the hills;
>
> And sometimes sent my ships in fleets
> All up and down among the sheets;

Or brought my trees and houses out,
And planted cities all about.

I was the giant great and still
That sits upon the pillow-hill,
And sees before him, dale and plain,
The pleasant land of counterpane.

The Robert Louis Stevenson poem gave him a way of looking at his confinement that made it more bearable, and the Victorian sensibility of my dad's formative years is clearly evident in the verse.

When arriving at my Grandmother Jewell's house, it was fun to go to Ma Bessie's room. She was always so delighted to see one of her great-grandchildren and there would inevitably be a game of Chinese checkers. She had a special table, the top of which was a Chinese checkers board. I think it was made of tin. The pattern on it was a colorful star shape, and each player sat at one of the points where a hollowed cup in the tin held their set of marbles. Ma Bessie's collection of marbles seemed like a coffer of jewels to me, though it was probably, in truth, kept in a cigar box. Each player enjoyed choosing their favorite kind of marble from among the glittery mix. One set was like knobby ivory, and the ones I liked best were of pink coral.

We also loved it when Grandmother Jewell brought Ma Bess to our house for a visit in her peacock blue and white Pontiac with magnificent chrome fins. David told me that they traveled like the Queen of Sheba. Ma Bess sat in the back and Jewell drove. In order to keep the Texas sun out, they would hang sections of deep blue cloth in the windows as curtains. Pop always worried because their view of the road was so badly obstructed. They brought along a special chair for Ma Bess, as well as a food grinder because, at her advanced age, she couldn't chew. Besides suitcases, they each had a cosmetic train case that seemed to be entirely full of interesting bottles and potions as well as delicious cough drops that Ma Bess let us have like candy.

On these visits, we all crowded into the kitchen as Jewell fried chicken for our dinner. Pop got Ma Bess and all of us children to laugh by making the telephone ring so that he could call his mother away to the phone and then ostentatiously steal a little piece of chicken, probably one of the livers or a wishbone piece, while she was gone.

Pop also used to tease his mother by calling the traditional Southern dishes she cooked Soul Food. She didn't appreciate him giving credit for her family recipes to a different cultural group, but he was right that the cuisine of Southern Black people and that of Southern whites were very much the same.

Bessie had married young and lost her husband to typhoid fever while still a youthful mother of three small children. She then went to live with her parents, but her father had died shortly thereafter. The female household carried on a gracious and civilized, though fairly impecunious, existence. Bessie's mother was the strict disciplinarian and head of the household, and Bessie's role was more that of a beloved and indulgent older sister to her children: Ella, Jewell, and Bobby. Bessie's mother took in boarders and continued to run the family store but did not make much of an income from these, mostly living on their garden and the chickens they kept. They clothed themselves in dresses they sewed for themselves and lace they tatted. My grandmother taught me how to tat, making lace from string wrapped in a particular way around your fingers, by making loops and knots with a kind of knitting motion. Quite difficult work.

Ma Bess annoyed my mother once when she revealed to us, her great-grandchildren, the existence of the Good Humor Man. She told us that if we heard some jingling music, we should get a nickel from our mother and run outside to get a frozen treat. Mother would have just as soon kept us in the dark about the Popsicle truck as long as possible. Ma Bess also annoyed my mother's mother when she called regularly just to say hello. Mammy never said Ma Bess was anything but pleasant; she just didn't feel like spending that much time "shooting the breeze" with John's grandmother.

There was a conspicuous difference between Ma Bessie's disposition and those of her frequently squabbling children. I get the impression that Bessie never tried to teach them how to behave; she was their benevolent child-mother. It speaks volumes about her charm and the influence of her loving nature that the three siblings, Ella, Jewell, and Bobby, who could never refrain from bickering with each other, never fussed at her, but only tried to outdo each other in serving and taking care of their mother.

Pop said that his usually cheerful grandmother could occasionally seem wistful and sad. He imagined Ma Bess was thinking of her young husband, lost to her long ago, but she never elaborated on it. She would only say, "I'm blue today."

5

Ampee

Jewell's sister, Ella, was called Ampee. She got her name from Pop's brother, Paul, when he was a very small boy and unable to pronounce "Auntie." The name stuck, and everyone, including her siblings, called her Ampee for the rest of her long life. She was quite a character and the name suited her. Ampee had very large eyes that were tremendously expressive. They could just as easily shine with joy, coyly flirt, or spit venom.

She always wore her hair in the style of her youth that most people today would recognize as Princess Leia cinnamon buns, but she had the style long before the princess. From my earliest recollection, Ampee had gray braids wound in the circular knots at her ears, held in place by large wavy hairpins made of pale golden tortoiseshell. The golden hairpins were a clue that her long braids had not always been gray, but might have once been blond.

In 1917, she went alone to Washington D.C. and got a job as an ace typist and stenographer, working for the War Department. She was self-sufficient and sent home money regularly. When Ampee met Uncle Al during the Depression, they decided to marry, but they kept their relationship a secret because during that time, only one government job was legally allowed per family.

As World War II got underway, Ampee was still in Washington, frequently sending home long typed letters. She became concerned about her younger nephew's ability to get on in the world if he couldn't type, and she wrote to someone in the military department that helped rehabilitate wounded soldiers. She asked if it was possible for soldiers who lost an arm in battle to learn how to type. The reply was encouraging and came with the recommendation of a typewriter with a specialized keyboard, which our dad's parents quickly acquired for young John and which would prove a great benefit to him.

Ampee's husband turned out to be a reprobate on several fronts. He drank and gambled and would sometimes ask his wife's relatives to lend him money. They often did so, but kept it secret from Ampee because they didn't want to hurt her feelings, even though they could ill afford the loss, as Al only rarely paid them back. So, when Ampee sent them money to help out, they were often only getting back some of the cash Uncle Al had cadged in the first place.

Al died before I was born. My brother, David, said Al died of cirrhosis of the liver, but sometimes David invented parts of stories to dramatize events and serve poetic truth. When Ampee retired, she moved back to Texas to live near her family. I never heard her say an unfavorable thing about Al, and she spoke of him often. She would refer to him as "Sweetie" and tell of adventures they had in our nation's capital. She was especially prone to talking about "Sweetie" at night when she took out her hairpins and her long gray braids came down to her waist over her girlish nightgown. It was her romantic adventure and she recalled it with delight. She would tell the story of driving to Delaware, where it was easy to get married and where they did not know anybody. They then lived together in D.C. when it was not known that they were married, rather risqué for the time. She also once told me about Uncle Al taking her to a burlesque house where there were ladies dancing on the stage "in their brassieres," which she remembered with sparkling eyes and blushes.

The decoration of Ampee's house was original, even eccentric. She had a large oil painting of a lion's head over the fireplace, and everywhere you looked, there were small ivory elephants, lined up on the mantle, on dressers, and on bookshelves. She collected these small elephants all her life, feeling an affinity for them because of her name, Ella.

When retired, the focus of her days was on gardening the large lot on which she had built her house. Whereas Jewell always hid from the sun beneath long gloves and parasols, Ampee worked in her yard and developed a permanent, deep brown tan. Her house in San Antonio was on the corner where Texas Avenue crossed Tulane Drive, and she never told you a house number when giving her address. She always just said, "Texas Avenue at Tulane." This sounded very elegant to her, and letters addressed in that way arrived just fine. She had an active imagination that led her to send letters to my brother addressed to Prince David, and to me addressed to Princess Rachel.

Nevertheless, Ampee was not just a sweet old lady. She had bars on her windows to protect her from burglars and she yelled at anyone who cut the corner and walked across her lawn. After being exasperated by children and mailmen who ignored her property line, she installed metal posts, a foot tall, along the perimeter with wire strung along the tops of them. Then, with a troll-like sense of glee, she sat back in her house and laughed and laughed when anyone tripped and went flying.

Ampee lived only a few blocks from Jewell, and they talked on the phone several times a day. A few doors down from Grandmother Jewell was a small grocery store that sent a delivery boy with anything she ordered over the phone, putting the cost on her account. Next to that was a wonderful old-fashioned drugstore, with its long counter and high stools to sit on. My siblings and I loved going there to order delicious malted milkshakes that we charged to Grandmother's account. Once we were told by Ampee to charge it to Mrs. Gralund. We were very confused and asked, "Who's she?" And that's when we learned her last name.

You would think that siblings who spent so much time together of their own free will would get along with each other, but these three squabbled incessantly. Ampee, Jewell, and Bobby had strong opinions about everything and they voiced them and badgered each other if there was not complete agreement. They could also attack anyone they thought had not behaved perfectly. Ampee, being the oldest, was the most vocal and the most domineering. Bobby spat back, refusing to be bullied, and he regularly teased Jewell for being too highfalutin. Jewell, the middle child, would put on a long-suffering air, fending Ampee and Bobby off with a sniff or making attacks in well-formed, holier-than-thou zingers. She was the immovable object to their unstoppable forces.

One episode of contention played out in letters between my dad and Ampee. These communications bring back all the asperity and domineering combativeness of her tone. My dad photocopied her letter, featuring run-on sentences, written in her 1985 Christmas card. Here it is:

You are all young, yet you made your 91 yr Mother come to the <u>cold Boston</u> and surrounding weather and leave we who are <u>old</u> and at this age to go this far as & especially when <u>so</u> few are left, you are <u>selfish</u> and young are the ones who should come to her – of course we don't count, you have a House full of young folks – so it makes a difference I guess. Anyway it isn't Xmas since Jewell is not here – at home with all of us – the few left –

Ampee 12-25-85

Then Pop replied, answering her charges against him. He wrote:

First of all, I did not make my ninety-year-old mother come to Boston for Christmas. I invited her to visit Boston on Thanksgiving. She agreed to do so and then she was talked out of coming by you. All had been prepared for her to visit us Thanksgiving and be back in Texas around the middle of December so that she could celebrate Christmas with you and Bob.

But you decided that she shouldn't travel anywhere and you harassed her until she canceled her trip. As a result, she missed the opportunity of taking photographs with all of our children and grandchildren, an occasion which rarely happens and will certainly not happen in Texas with nine members of our family and three grandchildren to make that possible. It is far more reasonable for my mother to fly to Boston than it is to fly twelve people to San Antonio.

He continued in the same vein to protest every charge. It indicates how forceful Ampee's accusations were in the family that he felt it necessary to defend himself point by point. Pop went on to write a newsy, friendly letter to Ampee, but he had called her out for hectoring his mother and him. A letter is actually the only way that this type of message could be gotten across to Ampee, because in person she would keep issuing angry declarations and you would never have a chance to fully state and argue your point.

When she was in a good humor, you would never guess that she could attack with such force. When her sister, Jewell, was not around to insist on the fundamentals, she indulged in reckless fun when playing cards with her great-nieces and David, her only great-nephew, making up new rules, usually involving lots of extra wild cards. Ampee was also a marvelous cook, specializing in yeasty, fresh rolls and homemade ice cream for special family dinners. It was always a good sign if you drove up to the house and she was outside, cranking away.

Though she was never a fashion plate, having been born in the 1890s she could not help having an old-fashioned sense of propriety and decorum. She certainly always thought she knew best and tried to impose her will on everyone. In the summer of 1972, our family spent several weeks in Austin, preparing our house there for renters. Pop, Mother, and the younger kids flew home to Boston, leaving the teenagers to drive back. Charles, whose family had lived next door, and whose parents had recently died leaving him in our care, was going, too, driving his own car along the same route. Then Ampee decided to go with us and surprise Pop. Maybe we should have kept the secret so Ampee could have surprised her nephew, but we called our dad on the phone and told him all about it before heading out because we were quite worried about her traveling at her age.

However, that was not what we should have been concerned about. She proved to be trouble right away. It was clear that she was not going to be just a happy passenger. She wanted to dictate plans, trying to eliminate some of the sights we would see on the pretext of saving time and our "father's gasoline."

She started in as soon as we picked her up in San Antonio, and by the time we were entering Austin two hours later she insisted that we stop at the Holiday Inn by the river, all together, and make our reservations for stops between Austin and Boston. She insisted that we could save some money if we made the trip in three days instead of four.

David and I had planned on dropping Ampee, Judith, and Alexandra off at the house while we went out to the Holiday Inn near there to make the reservations. (In those days, you didn't call ahead on the telephone. You went to a Holiday Inn to make reservations for the road ahead at other Holiday Inns in their network across the country.)

I finally gave up on politeness, as it was inevitably necessary to do when dealing with Ampee, and stated in no uncertain terms that that was how it was going to be. David and I had an ulterior motive that couldn't be stated. We wanted to get away and have a last cigarette before the long road trip.

There is a wonderful letter on Holiday Inn stationery that Ampee wrote two nights later to her sister and brother. It is full of vituper-ative accusations about me. Ampee makes me sound like the Queen of Hearts from *Alice's Adventures in Wonderland*. She wrote that I said, "This is my vacation and we are going to take four days and do what I want!" Then she continued, "…well it floored me when she said [that.] I have been nice and will continue but all that sweet palaver is mouth deep and in future I will take with a grain of salt. Don't fear. I have stayed out of any suggestions on anything."

Ampee also added that Alexandra had told her, "Rachel said that if I opened my mouth she'd tell Daddy that I complained." So I was the villain of the story Ampee sent home to San Antonio. But I have to trust that they knew Ampee well enough to take her word with "a grain of salt" as well.

We had wanted the trip to be a pleasant excursion, not just the shortest route between two points. It felt very shameful to have words with an eighty-something-year-old, but she could not stop her dom-ineering nature and I could not stand to be bulldozed. Finally, I left the problem with David and rode the rest of the way with Charles, avoiding more confrontation. As a teen, I always felt I was striving for independence, and I rebelled at constraints. At the time, I saw myself as very mature, leaving the family station wagon and riding off with Charles in his cool Chevy Nova, where I was free to smoke and we could stop at any spot that interested us along the way.

Ampee relaxed a bit and enjoyed the part of the trip in the Wash-ington D.C. area, her old stamping ground. When we walked around at Monticello, we saw two female tourists in quite short pants strolling by. Ampee's comment that we siblings have quoted ever since was, "The things you see when you don't have a gun!" We thought she made it up, but one of the characters said it in the BBC drama *Call the Midwife*, so perhaps it was a popular saying.

When we arrived in Boston, it didn't matter that we had not kept Ampee's surprise visit a secret. We didn't really spoil anything. It was still startling to see Ampee there in Boston, with her odd hairdo, baggy dress, and open-toed shoes, and she was delighted when Pop made much of her impromptu stowing away in our car to make the journey.

6

Uncle Bobby

Pop's Uncle Bobby never got over being the baby of the family. He cherished his reputation as a rebellious, happy-go-lucky jokester, and part of his rebellion, coming from a family of teetotalers, was to drink and work in a liquor store.

My grandmother maintained a disapproving attitude toward alcohol that only relaxed a little in her nineties when Pop introduced her to the sufficiently elegant Mandarine Napoléon. Her husband, Paul G., had made his own wine, but she never drank with him or even in her church, where they celebrated Holy Communion with grape juice rather than wine.

Throughout his life, Bobby rebelled against his strict upbringing in an environment that did not allow spirits, and he also rebelled against snooty attitudes wherever he found them. This was a continual clash for the siblings since Jewell's manner was ever superior and condescending.

I remember one particular Christmas, when my parents took us to spend the holidays with Grandmother Jewell. She had presents and stockings for all of us. The stockings contained the usual orange and small toys, along with samples from Crest that she had left over from the supply she gave out to her second-grade class. These included tablets you could dissolve in your mouth that left patches of color on spots that had plaque. I remember my brother and sisters and I all laughing at each other with bright pink lips and teeth, while Grandmother felt rather aggrieved that this ruined some of the photos. I also remember Grandmother gave each of her granddaughters a gold charm bracelet, each one different.

While we were occupied opening these presents, Uncle Bobby disappeared, only to return a little tipsy. His high spirits turned sour when it was clear that this part of the festivities was over and we were picking up discarded wrapping paper and moving toward the door. He sat there with his gifts, expecting to be the center of attention opening them, but we were all following Grandmother Jewell's lead and moving toward the kitchen to help serve Christmas dinner. This caused him to have a bit of a tantrum. "This is a hell of a note, and not very Christian of you to treat me like I'm not even one of the family," he called out belligerently to his sister.

Jewell got the pained expression on her face that bickering with her siblings always caused. She was probably most injured because he had been imbibing, but she didn't mention that. He then went out again, I imagine to his work room in the garage, where he very likely took another little swig. When we were seated at Christmas dinner, he reappeared, his good spirits restored, carrying in a pan of dinner rolls that Grandmother had intentionally left in the kitchen because they were burned. Uncle Bobby waltzed in, calling out, "Anyone for chocolate rolls?"

My dad remembered Uncle Bobby always being a sympathetic ally. One time when his Aunt Margaret came for a visit, she brought a brand-new bicycle for Paul, but nothing for Johnny. Uncle Bobby took his younger nephew aside and told him, "I'm gonna get you a brand-new bike." Johnny knew he wouldn't but appreciated his heartfelt concern.

The bicycle event was so meaningful in our dad's life that he tried to recreate it in different ways for his children. He seemed to feel that it was important for each child to experience a sense of unfairness and to suffer from it, followed by a communing moment with someone who understood. My turn to become initiated in this ritual occurred over an actual bicycle when I was eight years old.

While visiting San Antonio one autumn, our cousins, Paulette and Susanne, gave us their very pretty old bicycles. On our return home, the bicycles disappeared for a while only to turn up, freshly cleaned and polished under the Christmas tree. They were metallic blue, and the slightly larger one had hand brakes. As children we always lined up on the stairs in descending order, from the oldest down to the youngest at the foot of the stairs, to be photographed before entering the living room to see what Santa Claus had brought. As soon as I rounded the corner and saw the bicycles, I knew the larger one had to be for me. I crossed the room and pulled the tag toward me. It was in disbelief that I read my sister Judith's name. My first thought was that there was some mistake; in my mind she was supposed to have the smaller bike. Perhaps the tags got switched. I looked at the tag on the smaller bicycle and read my sister Alexandra's name, with an awful wave of misery gushing through me.

As the joyous present opening progressed all around, I would go back to the bikes several times and look at the tags again and again to make sure my name wasn't there somewhere, that the tag didn't say "and Rachel" on the other side. I must have received other gifts, but I don't remember them. My mind was in a fog thinking about the bicycle that wasn't mine. At last my dad called out to me, "Rachel, there's something you overlooked." There was a card tucked into the branches of the tree with my name on it, and it was attached to a string. I took the strand and followed it crazily around the edge of the room and out the door, where it led down the hall and under the door to the back porch. When I pulled open that door, there was a shiny, new, black English Racer. I still feel that explosion of joy as I remember finding my beautiful bicycle. My parents did love me. I hadn't been forgotten after all.

Pop loved Uncle Bobby for being on his side and for trying to cheer him up when he was hurt, but there were other ways he learned from his uncle, as well. During the Depression, Uncle Bobby mowed the lawn and did other handyman jobs for his sister, Jewell. She always paid him with a pack of cigarettes. Once, when he had finished the day's work and Grandmother was handing him the Chesterfields, she admonished him, "Don't smoke them up too quickly." Bobby turned on her and threw the pack back in her face. Pop admired Uncle Bobby enormously at that moment. Yes, he did menial jobs for his sister, but he didn't take this high-handed and insulting order from her.

Although Uncle Bobby maintained a room at Ampee's house, he usually lived at Jewell's after my grandfather died. Being very much the Southern belle, she never spent a night in a house alone in all her ninety-eight years. When we were young, each of us grandchildren took turns visiting Grandmother Jewell on our own. From the time I was in third grade, I could ride the Greyhound bus from Austin to San Antonio to see her. The short visits were filled with trips to the San

Antonio Zoo, shopping at Joske's, and dining on delicious Mexican food at the old La Fonda on Main.

Visiting Grandmother on our own gave us each a chance to really absorb her milieu for a few days. Everything was done at a slow deliberate pace; there was none of the rough and tumble atmosphere that was inevitable in our world at home with seven children. At Grandmother Jewell's you always put almond-scented lotion on your hands after washing them, and when you were going to help cook, you tied back your hair with a scarf. Uncle Bobby was a counterpoint to this staid atmosphere. He cracked jokes, whistled to get your attention, and ostentatiously put hot sauce on the mildly seasoned food Jewell cooked.

Uncle Bobby participated in these visits in other ways, too. On my first trip alone, he stopped by the drugstore on his way home from work and brought me chocolates and perfume. The scent was called Evening in Paris, and it came in a beautiful cobalt-blue bottle. As a third grader, I had never gotten such an elegant gift before. While Jewell prepared dinner, Uncle Bobby and I liked to watch *Five Star Shock* on television. Each episode was a mild thriller that might involve a giant, trained ape, or mad scientist, or both. Austin only had one television station then, so San Antonio's three stations seemed luxurious. Uncle Bobby also had a wooden birdhouse that had three slotted rooms, open on one side. He kept several tins of paint in his workroom and always let his visiting grandnieces or grandnephew paint the birdhouse however they liked, right over the last masterpiece.

There is an old photograph of Uncle Bobby standing against a car, with his two nephews on either side of him. They are all grinning and relaxed, Johnny and Paul leaning up against their uncle affectionately.

Bobby was well-liked wherever he went. Waitresses remembered him and greeted him in a friendly manner, and when he was unwell at the end of his life, the nurses and attendants at the nursing home doted on him with genuine warmth. Of course, liquor was strictly forbidden in that environment, but that didn't stop Paul from taking his uncle a small bottle of Old Grand-Dad. Paul tells it that Uncle Bobby's eyes lit up as he cracked the bottle open and took a healthy swig. Smiling broadly, he let out a sound of appreciation, "Ahhhh," then looking at Paul, he said, "The good stuff," and died. A droll humorist to the end.

7

Paul

Paul took his younger brother under his wing from day one, calling Johnny "Sug," like the first syllable of sugar. It is not certain who originated the nickname; at any rate, both Paul and Uncle Bobby called Johnny Sug, and the name perfectly expresses the special love and steadfast concern they felt for him. Some boys don't like to have a younger brother tagging along everywhere, but Paul accepted Sug as his comrade in every youthful endeavor, from digging in the backyard, to climbing trees. And young Sug was determined to keep up.

When baby John was born with a deformed arm, his mother was in shock at first, but Paul G. convinced Jewell that they must focus on making the most of what their baby had. Pop said his parents were determined to make his life as normal as possible, so they never stopped him from things other boys did, even though they had to hold their breath sometimes with worry.

His mother shortened his right sleeves to just above his stub, shaped like a fist-sized ball with a smaller ball set askew on top of it. The stub wasn't hidden so that he could use it as much as possible like a hand. He was able to bend it, hang from it, grip things with it, and even fight with it. So far as I could tell, Pop never resented a more ideal human form. In fact, he revered it, and I think his passionate interest in art and sculpting grew from that reverence.

As a result of his upbringing, Pop always seemed capable of anything. It never occurred to us, his children, that he was disabled in any way. Pop once overheard me telling another small child matter-of-factly that my dad had one regular arm and one "ball arm." It seemed as simple as that. We found that Pop's old shirts made excellent smocks for painting. We only had to roll up one of the sleeves because the other one was altered to the correct length. When we were children, we did acrobatics with him, holding onto his hand and his stub, and then, part jumping and part being lifted by Pop, we flew up to stand on his shoulders. His belief in his own ability, always ready to try new things, is probably attributable to his constant play with Paul, and in his brother insisting that the neighborhood boys accepted Sug in all their games as well.

Johnny felt that Paul was infallible, and he learned attentively from him. Once, their father gave them the job of emptying the very large planter in the front yard. This ornate cement vessel decorated in sculpted detail was larger than the young boys combined, and Paul had the idea that they could empty it a lot faster with a small explosion. With Sug following him and observing every move, Paul went to where his father kept a gun. Pop remembered very clearly watching Paul as he showed his little brother where the safety catch was, making sure it was set, and then opening the gun and showing Sug the bullets, taking them out and putting them back in before closing up the gun again. Paul then took a few bullets from the box that was stored with the gun and showed Johnny how to open them up and pour out the gunpowder.

The boys then put the gunpowder in the urn, attached a homemade fuse to it, and lit it. With a huge blast, the dirt flew everywhere, emptying the planter, but also breaking it into several pieces. Of course, the brothers were punished, but they never learned to be contrite for what they had done. I once remarked that Paul could have gotten them both badly hurt by handling a gun and taking apart bullets. However, Pop maintained that Paul knew what he was doing.

In a few notable instances, Sug could not follow in his brother's footsteps. When Paul joined the army during World War II, young Johnny went to a recruiting office and tried to join as well, but he was too young to join without his parents' permission and they refused. So Sug stayed in San Antonio going to college while Paul served in the Pacific theater. Paul came back severely injured. When a shell exploded, his chest took a hit. David once told me that when Uncle Paul breathed in, most of his chest expanded, but there was a part where the scar was that didn't move. I never saw this myself, but we were all properly awed by how close our family had come to losing him. Paul also came back changed in other ways. He was more worldly and independent of his parents' influence.

Shortly after Paul's recovery, he married Phyllis Hayden, a fellow student of my parents at Trinity University. Phyllis had, in fact, gone out on a few dates with Johnny before meeting Paul on his return from the war. Pop was always fond of Phyllis and would sometimes remind her that he had known her longer than his brother had. Paul and Phyllis decided on a small wedding, and they didn't invite his parents to attend. Jewell felt especially hurt by this stinging insult, but Paul was a young G.I. and he wanted to celebrate with his friends and serve alcohol, which he knew his mother would not countenance.

The age of Victorian rectitude in which Jewell grew up included temperance, and for her, drinking was equated with wickedness. Independence from this heritage required the constant need to reassert one's self. Even for Paul's daughters, my cousins, setting boundaries and shaking off old-world imperatives was a struggle. Once, Ampee visited my cousin Paulette and noticed an old-fashioned wooden icebox. She had a fit when she opened it and found that my cousin used it as a liquor cabinet.

Pop didn't side with Paul when he excluded the older generation from his wedding. He felt bad for his parents and didn't think the slight was necessary. However, Paul established his autonomy, which was especially important to him since he remained in San Antonio, near to his parents, all his life. Paul, as an engineer, even became a partner in business with his father, the architect, for a while. Pop told me there was a period of about a year or so when Paul and their dad did not speak to each other, but that they mostly got along working in the same office.

Paul G. was a Freemason, and Paul Jr. joined the fraternal order as well. Once again, young John could not follow his brother. Only this time, he was refused because of his disabled arm. When, as a teenager, I asked my dad why he wasn't a Mason even though Uncle Paul and Granddaddy were, I was astounded when he told me that he had been excluded for that reason. It hadn't occurred to me before that he had suffered any ostracism on account of his stub. I asked him if he felt outraged at being rejected, but he told me that he got over it a long time ago, and he believed he took a better path.

Paul became a representative to the Texas State Legislature in 1970, and he ran again in 1972 when I was in high school. It was my first experience being involved in a political campaign. On Election Day, I was dropped off at one of the polling stations, where I stood holding a sign and asking people to vote for my uncle until I was picked up by my cousin, Susanne, in the evening. It is very grueling work standing outside for hours like that, but I was only sorry I wasn't given any Silber Dollars to hand out. Uncle Paul's team had created some large silver coins that said *Silber Dollar* on one side and *Vote for Paul Silber* on the other. They were the coolest political souvenir I ever saw.

For us, this was a foretaste of what it would be like when Pop ran for governor of Massachusetts in 1990. During his elections and while he was in office, Paul conferred regularly with Pop. Paul's main focus was on education, a shared interest of the brothers. It was disappointing when Paul lost his seat in his second run. Pop said it was because the boundaries of the district had been changed.

When Paul and his family visited us in Boston, Boston University friends were always surprised at how similar the brothers looked, though Pop was a few inches taller and his hair had darkened over the years while Paul's had turned to silver. Paul enjoyed telling our friends that they could easily tell the brothers apart, as he was the one "who doesn't use Color Comb."

He had another ploy he liked to use on those who were not too well-acquainted with Pop. When they approached Paul at the post-graduation party, saying, "Pleased to meet you, President Silber," he'd grin, hold out his right hand, and wait for the realization to set in.

As much as my dad admired Paul's ability as a huntsman and his proper care of guns, he never felt comfortable with the casual acquaintance with guns that Paul's family had. Pop practiced marksmanship and sometimes took us target shooting, and, as a security measure, he kept a gun in his bedroom in a safe with a combination lock. This was nothing compared to Paul's extensive gun collection, and it was known among the family that Aunt Phyllis often carried a gun under the seat of her car or in her purse. She also had a temper on occasion and was much stricter than our mother. Phyllis was beautiful and had black hair with a widow's peak that David pointed out was very much like that of the wicked queen, Maleficent, in *Sleeping Beauty*. Pop sometimes teased Paul that he expected someday to hear Phyllis had shot him.

The use of cell phones changed everything for the brothers. They could once more talk to each other several times a day, a real comfort to them in their old age. Paul would generally ring Sug when he was taking his walk to help pass the time, and anytime something amusing happened, John would telephone Paul, whom he usually called "Pablo," just to share a laugh with him. During Pop's final illness, Paul made the trip to Boston to visit with him and help us talk him into trying a few weeks of rehab to build up his strength, as always, watching out for Sug.

Big brother Paul and young Johnny. Notice Paul's frilly collar and John's curls. Their mother, Jewell, had gotten some ideas from the book *Little Lord Fauntleroy*. Silber Family Photos.

Top: Jewell at home in Cameron, Texas, with her mother, Ma Bess, and her grand-mother, Granny Robertson. *Bottom:* Jewell driving the little coupe Paul G. gave her when they were first married, 1923. Silber Family Photos.

Top: Paul G. and Jewell with Paul and John posing with the infamous planter—the brothers would later blow it up with gunpowder and a fuse. *Bottom:* The brothers, John and Paul, in knickerbockers. Silber Family Photos.

Top: JRS and another Boy Scout, with two girls, feasting on watermelon. *Bottom:* Brothers Paul and John, in their Boy Scout uniforms, 1940. Silber Family Photos.

Top: Paul and John with Ma Bess in 1943. *Bottom:* Paul and John with their Uncle Bobby. You can see how fond they are of him. Silber Family Photos.

Top: Kathryn's father, Harvey Underwood, in France, 1917. *Bottom:* Kathryn with her dog Kleenex—back when paper handkerchiefs were a new and exciting thing. Silber Family Photos.

Top: Mary Underwood, AKA "Mammy," with Kathryn and her brother Bill in Normanna, Texas. *Bottom:* Kathryn in a field with her hat at a rakish angle. Silber Family Photos.

Left: John and Kathryn look like they are doing a dance number in a 1940s musical. *Right:* Dick and Jean Rossbacher, housemates with John and Kathryn at Yale and lifelong friends. Silber Family Photos.

An early selfie! John photographs Kathryn and himself looking in the mirror at a diner. Silber Family Photos.

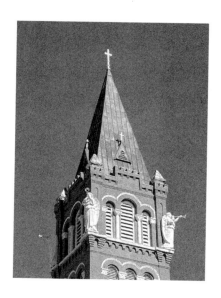

Top: Trumpeting angels on the four corners of the steeple, sculpted by Pop's father, Paul G. Silber, at the University of the Incarnate Word in San Antonio, Texas. Photo by Caroline Silber Lavender. *Bottom:* JRS studied sculpting with Pompeo Coppini. Pop often took us to see this fountain sculpted by Coppini at U.T. Austin. Notice the mermen are riding horses with webbed hooves. Photo by John Silber.

48

Top: Kathryn and John with baby David. They look like they are taking their new responsibility seriously! *Bottom:* Kathryn holding Rachel as David makes her laugh. I like to think of Pop capturing this moment on film. Silber Family Photos.

Top: Paul G. Silber with his grandson, David. *Bottom:* Rachel and David. Some of my hair is pulled back to the side with a rubber band. We used to call this having my hair "in a feather." Silber Family Photos.

Top: A thoughtful profile of Jewell, with me looking over Ma Bessie's shoulder; David smiles for the camera; Judith almost in the picture. In this picture you can see how much fun Ma Bessie was. I think of Pop taking most of these pictures. *Bottom:* Alexandra, Rachel, David, Judith, and Martha. You can see where the burnt part of the photo had to be cut away. We lost many photos in the fire at Carlton Street. Silber Family Photos.

Top: Judith, Rachel, and David, Christmas 1958. Judith and I are fascinated by my new Betsy Wetsy. This photo appeared in the *Austin American-Statesman*. *Bottom:* Judith, David, Alexandra, and Rachel, Germany 1960. Judith and I are in identical outfits, but I had been playing in the woods. It also looks like I might be in trouble for coming home late. Silber Family Photos.

Top: Rachel, Judith, and David, Germany 1960. Judith got a birthday cake topped with marzipan mushrooms. *Bottom:* Rachel, Judith, JRS, Frau Anderseck holding Alexandra, David, and Kathryn on a gondola in Venice, 1959.
Silber Family Photos.

Top: Martha with our Cadillac limousine. As always, with a luggage rack when on vacation. *Bottom:* Jewell, David, Martha, Kathryn, Ruth, Alexandra, Judith, and Ampee in our Austin dining room. The painting on the wall, called *Father and Son*, is by Don Weismann. Sadly, it and others were burned in the fire at the Carlton Street house soon after we arrived in Boston. Silber Family Photos.

Top: Mother in the back seat of our Cadillac limousine looking very glamorous in her sunglasses, but on a cross-country trip she probably had a diaper pail near her feet. *Bottom:* Cousin Susanne Silber Schieffer behind the wheel of her new Fiat, in Grandmother Jewell's driveway with Uncle Bobby, Christmas 1968.
Silber Family Photos.

Top: Laura Ruth, Caroline, JRS, Martha, David, and Alexandra. Standing behind are Kathryn, Judith, and Rachel, on our eating porch in Austin, 1969. *Bottom:* David with Judith, who is showing off her sunglasses. Silber Family Photos.

Top: Laura Ruth, David, Caroline, Alexandra, and Kathryn aboard the *DRAMJACKYL*. *Bottom:* Alexandra, David, Caroline, Laura Ruth, JRS, and Judith aboard the *DRAMJACKYL*, 1970. Silber Family Photos.

Top: Candid shot of John Silber being interviewed for the job as president of Boston University, gesturing with his large left hand. Boston University Photography.
Bottom: The photographer, Leo Touchet, got up on a ladder to take this picture of us for *Life* magazine, 1971. Copyright 2022 Leo Touchet.

The Boston University search committee, presided over by Trustees Chairman
Hans Estin and charged with finding a new president, made up of trustees, administration, professors, and students—as *Life* magazine put it in the article title, it was
a "Quest for a Silver Unicorn: Boston University's Long Search for a New President," *Life* magazine, June 4, 1971.
Ralph Morse/The LIFE Picture Collection/Shutterstock.

Top: Mammy and Jewell flew to Boston to join us for Pop's inauguration, 1971.
Front row: Mammy, Kathryn, Ruth, JRS, Jewell, and David holding Caroline.
Back row: Martha, Alexandra, Rachel, and Judith. *Bottom:* Exterior view of the
Silber House on Carlton Street in Brookline on December 22, 1971.
Boston University Photography.

Photo of John taken by Kathryn on our ski trip to Sugarbush, December 1971.
Little did we know that an arsonist was setting fire to the house on Carlton Street
while we were away. Silber Family Photos.

Top: Formal family photograph in the front hall at Carlton Street. *Bottom:* Portrait of Kathryn Silber in the living room at Carlton Street, November 28, 1971. Boston University Photography.

Top: Uncle Paul imitating the hoity-toity manner he claims his brother, John, has acquired now that he lives in Boston. Silber Family Photos. *Bottom:* Grandmother Jewell in the living room at the Carlton Street house.
Boston University Photography.

Top, left to right: Administration vs. Security softball game: Bill Bennett, Ernie Corvo, Ed Penn, and JRS. *Center:* JRS at bat. *Bottom:* JRS had a way of fielding the ball, quickly whipping off his glove, and then throwing.
Boston University Photography.

Top: JRS with his typically overloaded desk. Paul J. Connell for the *Boston Globe.*
Bottom: JRS speaking at Commencement. Boston University Photography.

Top: President Silber with Tip O'Neill before the BU Commencement on May 20, 1973. *Bottom:* President Silber with Senator Ed Brook before the Commencement on May 29, 1974. Boston University Photography.

Top: President Silber with Julia Child before the BU Commencement on May 23, 1976. *Bottom:* JRS with Spencer Frankl, a great friend, a great and gentle dentist, and a great lover of music, at the garden party at Carlton Street after Commencement, May 22, 1977. Boston University Photography.

Top: President John Silber honors Ella Fitzgerald at Commencement on Nickerson Field, May 21, 1978. *Bottom:* President Silber with Arthur Metcalf and Clare Boothe Luce at the Boston University Commencement in Heidelberg, 1979. Boston University Photography.

Top: JRS lights Red Auerbach's cigar on the Commencement platform, 1984. *Bottom:* Clara Hale, often called Mother Hale, founded Hale House where she made a home for children born with AIDS or drug addiction. President Silber presents Hale with an honorary degree, in 1987, attended by Trustee Suzanne Cutler. Boston University Photography.

Top: Chief Justice of the Supreme Court William Rehnquist (*middle*) with Trustee Earle Cooley and JRS in 1987. *Bottom:* Opera singer and College of Fine Arts Dean Phyllis Curtin speaks at the College of Fine Arts Commencement at the Boston University Theatre on Huntington Ave., 1988.
Boston University Photography.

Top: President Silber with Carl Yastrzemski at the post-Commencement garden party at the house on Carlton Street on May 15, 1988. *Bottom:* Christopher Ricks (*left*), honored with the Metcalf Cup and Prize for excellence in teaching, 1990. Attended by Trustee Chairman Arthur Metcalf.
Boston University Photography.

Top: JRS with Lieutenant General William P. Yarborough, known as "Father of the Modern Green Berets." *Bottom:* Elma Lewis with JRS. Lewis was a Boston University graduate and founder of the Elma Lewis School of Fine Arts. Boston University Photography.

Top: Velia Tosi and Kathryn at a Boston University Women's Council meeting at the Carlton Street house. *Bottom:* President Silber stops to talk with students on the steps of Hayden Hall. Boston University Photography.

Top: JRS arguing with a group of students at Senior Breakfast, 1972.
Bottom: JRS uses a bullhorn to be heard at a protest.
Boston University Photography.

JRS makes the 205th annual Municipal Oration to Boston officials at Faneuil Hall, 1976. His speech was called "Democracy: Its Counterfeits and Its Promise." Boston University Photography.

Top: Faculty strike, American Association of University Professors, 1979.
Center: Faculty strike at Boston University, 1979. *Bottom:* JRS interviewed about
the faculty strike by Joe Day with WCVB in 1979.
Boston University Photography.

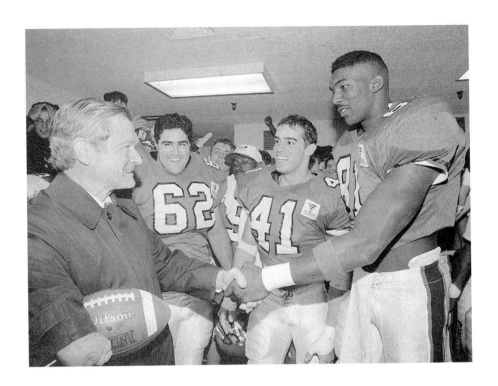

Top: President Silber is given the game ball after the homecoming victory on October 23, 1993. Photo by Kalman Zabarsky for Boston University Photography.
Bottom: President Silber with Boston University mascot Rhett the Terrier at a buffet for student leaders, 1984. Boston University Photography.

Top: JRS with grandson John at a Boston University football game.
Bottom: Anti-apartheid demonstration during the visit of Chief Mangosuthu Buthelezi in 1986. Boston University Photography.

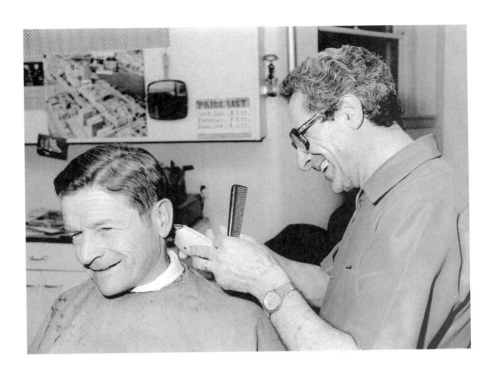

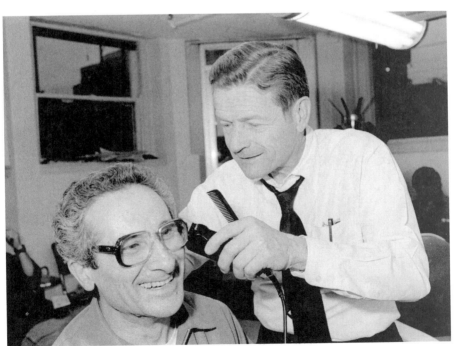

Top: John Zizza, longstanding barber of John Silber, at University Barber Shop cutting Silber's hair. *Bottom:* John Silber trimming John Zizza's hair. Pop was actually a very good barber. Boston University Photography.

Top: Ruth at breakfast in "the eating porch" at Carlton Street. Silber Family Photos.
Bottom: Kathryn and John pose for a photo with their well-worn copy of *The Joy of Cooking* for the Boston University cookbook *Cooking by Degrees*.
Boston University Photography.

PART TWO

Foreground

From Texas to Boston and How We Lived There

8

Kathryn

I THINK OF MY MOTHER PRIMARILY AS A READER. SHE CONSUMED books of all kinds, ravenously, all her life. When we were young, she took us on weekly visits to the library, from which she always brought home a pile of books for herself. I recognized the skull and cross-bones on the spines of the mysteries, but the others were inscrutable to me. It seemed to me like she simply wanted to read every book ever written.

She once said that if nothing else was available she would have to read the labels on canned goods and medicine bottles. When Grand-mother Jewell, in her late nineties, came to stay for several months, her eyes had weakened to the point that she could no longer read. It was winter and she longed to see the snow, but when it came, she stared out the window but wasn't able to see it. David and I found that most poignant, but Mother was more troubled by the idea of not being able to read. She thought that if she were ever in that predicament she would have to learn Braille.

Kathryn also liked to show off, habitually doing the *New York Times* crossword puzzle in ink. Another example of this exhibitionism occurred when she was staying with me after my daughter, Mary Beth, was born. On that visit, she read a huge book each day, alternating fiction and nonfiction.

She could be quite contemptuous if one of us, her children, did not know a historical fact or reference she felt we should know. And yet she never told us to read or study or really to do anything. She believed wholeheartedly in teaching by example, with each of us having the free will to follow or not.

This method included always speaking to us politely. I don't think I ever heard her raise her voice at anyone, which is something of a tri-umph when you have seven children. It is also quite astonishing when you consider that she was married to a man who regularly spoke his mind vociferously. Argument was his customary reaction if he thought something wasn't right. Pop felt that debate, even heated debate, was the best way to teach. Get all the disagreements out on the table, blow the roof off with intense discussion, and come to some truth in the end. In this arena of clashing styles they were worthy adversaries because Kathryn had a sure advantage: humor. A master of the quick, sharp rejoinder, she could dispel a dark mood and have them both laughing. Once she had him laughing close to tears when she replied to his less than favorable comment with, "I guess I should have expected a left-handed compliment like that from you." Then Pop had to explain to us kids what a left-handed compliment was and why it was funny.

Although our dad was a few months older than our mother when they met at Trinity University, he was a new freshman and she was a year ahead of him. She showed him the ropes, calling him "Son," and he called her "Ma." Johnny was a handsome boy and well-liked. Among many other activities and enthusiasms, he developed an interest in hypnotism during this time and practiced on my mother and several of her friends, keeping detailed notes of each experiment. Uncle Bill, my mother's brother, always maintained that Kathryn was putting on an act when John hypnotized her, but if that was the case, she never admitted it.

Bill didn't like this strange young man with a short right arm coming to the house with his notebook and self-important claim of being able to mesmerize Kathryn. The fact that he could induce her to go along and pretend to succumb made it even worse. Bill was younger than Kathryn, but he was, even then, a hulking six foot three, and his instinctive response was to clobber the little upstart. All of Pop's experience fighting in the schoolyard came to the fore and he fought Bill like his life depended on it. And it probably did. How could Kathryn respect him if her little brother whipped the stuffing out of him? The two boys didn't hold back, and both got in plenty of punches, but once they were down on the ground Pop rolled right on top of Bill and, with his stub, his secret weapon with its sharp-edged bone, he pummeled his attacker's kidneys until he started howling. Mammy ran out of the house to find out what the commotion was and sized up the situation immediately. Both boys were filthy and smeared with blood, but Kathryn's caller was winning. All Mammy said was, "Okay, John, rub his face in the dirt, and let that be an end to it."

After a while, John and Kathryn became debate partners, competing in tournaments and winning several trophies. Pop often described how pretty Mother was when she debated, taking it all very seriously and holding her hands in a certain way to emphasize each point. When he ran for governor of Massachusetts, he said that the way she made campaign speeches reminded him very much of the way she debated. He thought she looked so attractive in her pretty dresses, facing each audience earnestly while accentuating every point in her talk with her characteristic, graceful hand gestures. Throughout the years, Kathryn did quite a lot of public speaking, whether on a stage, at a podium, or at a dinner table making a toast. Pop was always proud of her intelligence, refined manner, and most of all of her humor. He never tried to tell her what to say or vet her remarks in advance, and often he was surprised and delighted by what she came up with.

At an august gathering of the American Institute of Architects in 2002, when Pop was given the distinction of being named an honorary member, there were many speakers who praised his abiding interest in architecture and his attention to every detail of the buildings constructed at Boston University. Toward the end of the evening, it was my mother's turn to speak, a difficult place in the lineup of eloquent speakers, all extolling her husband's virtues. What more could she add? She rose from her table and went to the podium on the stage, where she spoke into the microphone; "My mother always told me that if you can't say something nice, don't say anything." The audience went wild with laughter and applause.

The college years were very simple, innocent times for young John and Kathryn. They were very busy with classes and clubs and their many friends. None of these kids had much money, but they could buy a bowl of chili at the Mexican restaurant near campus for a nickel, and free tortillas came with it. Mother and her most intimate group of girlfriends developed a rather racy game. Each one chose a candidate, and the object of the game was to get married first. Kathryn won. When my parents got married, each of them just twenty years old, shortly after John graduated in 1947, they were naturally eager to get to the St. Anthony Hotel and cohabit for the first time, but years later, they also remembered the fun, as husband and wife, of going out for ice cream sodas first thing after the wedding reception.

Kathryn always thought pillows were a great luxury, never having had one as a child. My siblings and I each had our own small, child-sized pillow, and when attending a baby shower, her favorite present to give was a small down pillow with pretty pillowcases. Even after this was considered a no-no for babies, she continued the practice. It wasn't that she hadn't heard any warnings; she simply didn't believe them. Her other favorite gift, this one for children, was a pocket knife. We children always had pocket knives, and I remember cutting a finger more than once while using mine. When we got older, our parents gave us Swiss Army knives. Every day, Pop would pull out his own pocket knife to cut open letters or packages, and Mother usually carried a small one in her purse. She once had to hand her knife over to security before boarding a flight because she had forgotten to take it out and leave it at home.

Kathryn was skeptical of all official rules and strictures on any subject. She felt it was essential to live life by your own beliefs and values. She bridled at the intrusion of schools into our lives, and though, when necessary, she would write the required note to have us released early from class, she refused to give a specific reason. Her note might simply say, "Please excuse Rachel at one o'clock. She is needed at home." As she got older, she made it clear to her daughters that no matter how ill she became, she would never submit to living in a nursing home. As she put it, "I would rather die on my own kitchen floor."

Most of her ailments resulted from smoking cigarettes, a habit she enjoyed tremendously as a perfect complement to reading. Although Pop never became a regular cigarette smoker, he developed a fondness for cigars. Some of the most convivial images of my parents, captured in my memory, are of the two sitting together, he with a cigar, and she with a cigarette, perhaps alfresco, enjoying a pleasant afternoon, or at a table after a meal.

To me, the image of a man and a woman smoking together epitomized elegance. Did I get that idea from my parents or from the movies? The most famous example would be Bogart and Bacall, but my favorite screen romance involving cigarettes was between Barbara Stanwyck and Dennis Morgan in *Christmas in Connecticut*. I love the way she lights his cigarette as he plays the piano next to the Christmas tree. As a teenager, I felt smoking was a rite of passage toward sophisticated adulthood.

Mother usually read to us at bedtime when we were quite young. She would read anything we wanted, but some of the books were chosen by her. One of my earliest memories is of being read Bible stories, where I learned that my brother's name was biblical, from the great story of David and Goliath. Around the same time she read us the Uncle Remus stories, which we loved. This book is now dated and considered racist by some, but my experience of it was of a kindly Black uncle, telling stories of fantastic and clever wildlife characters. The language that the old man used was in dialect, and Mother told us he spoke that way because he never had a chance to go to school. It seemed like a valuable lesson, that someone might tell the best stories and have a great imagination even if they were from a different race, background, or class. In hindsight, I also suspect that my mother might have omitted any offensive words that she didn't want us to hear or learn.

Some friends once gave us a book of manners for children that we thought was the most hilarious book ever written. When Mother read it, we would roll around laughing. This usually took place on the couch in the living room where we lolled or perched, clean sweet-smelling children, fresh from our baths, wearing our pajamas. Mother sat at the end, next to the table where the lamp seemed to shed a golden light on us, and Pop would come in and look on.

Mother read to us only because we were young and didn't know how, but she didn't really like to read aloud. Pop loved being read to; the favorite teachers he recalled from school were the ones who read aloud to the class. Perhaps it had something to do with her quick brain, or the intimate relationship she liked to have with a book that caused her to dislike the slower pace and shared experience. Pop would have gladly read to her; however, for the same reasons, she felt an antipathy for that as well. When we children were a bit older, Pop read aloud to us, often from classics or old favorites he found in used book stores. I remember the fun of him reading *King Solomon's Mines*. Allan Quatermain traversing the snow-topped mountains called Sheba's Breasts seemed rather risqué and romantic to my young mind. Later, when *The Sword in the Stone* came out in movie theaters, Pop read us *The Once and Future King*.

At Yale, John and Kathryn shared graduate-student housing with another couple, Dick and Jean Rossbacher. Made cheaply, with paper-thin walls, the layout of their unit had separate living quarters for each couple, with a shared kitchen in between. One night, John realized that from their apartment, he could hear Dick and Jean reading aloud to each other, something he soon discovered they did every evening. From then on, Pop would quietly curl up beside the shared wall and listen to them read each evening. I'm sure my mother would not have approved of this eavesdropping, but she didn't try to stop him. Luckily, when my dad finally confessed what he had been doing, Dick and Jean good-naturedly accepted it, and the four became lifelong friends, often spending vacation time together with their children for many years to come.

Mother became a marvelous cook, always preparing great quantities for our large family, and as there was plenty, Pop could bring someone home for dinner on the spur of the moment. We often had very different picnic-style meals when Pop traveled, a favorite being BLTs and chocolate shakes made in the blender, or hot dogs fried in bacon grease with mustard and ketchup added right in the frying pan. It was fun letting our hair down, and I was sorry Pop wasn't in on these casual feasts. Pop missed that side of things, but he was the master of impromptu late-night grilled cheese sandwiches with tomato slices and oregano that he and Mother enjoyed on occasion.

Mother was an intensely private person, and when we moved to Boston, she found it difficult to develop anything resembling a cozy friendship. I feel she was warm with most people but not confidential. She didn't divulge any secrets. It was extra hard to make close friends in this new situation where she and Pop were very much in the public eye, where she felt she had very little privacy. She enjoyed the university social occasions, but it was not easy for her to relax and casually enjoy another person on an intimate level. The exception was Mary Finn, who got past Kathryn's reserve by not seeming to notice it. Also, they just clicked. Mary was married to Dan Finn, a Boston University vice president, and living very close to the president's house, she started dropping by to chat or ask Kathryn to join her taking a walk around the neighborhood. Mary was unpretentious and easy, forthright, sporty, and even girlish in her manner. A great deal of joy was stolen from Mother's world when, after knowing one another for only a few years, Mary died suddenly from a severe asthma attack.

Our parents had been married for fifty-seven years at the time of Kathryn's death. Nevertheless, John was surprised by how much he had depended on her. Even though they worked as a team, he had maintained an image of them as two strong, self-sufficient people. He didn't realize how much he relied on her until she was gone.

During the lonely time that followed, he would often attempt the *New York Times* crossword puzzle, and when Martha or I were there, or when another sibling was visiting, he would ask us to help. He never got close to completing one, usually only filling in part of one quadrant, but the ritual was a kind of paying homage to Kathryn.

9

Six Daughters

PEOPLE ALWAYS SAY THAT WE LOOK ALIKE, AND THAT MAY BE. WE are, nevertheless, six fundamentally disparate individuals. Some hold the theory that we developed that way in order to distinguish ourselves from one another. However, as the oldest girl, born twenty-two months after David, the only boy, I was there and can attest that each of my younger sisters was born with her own fully formed personality. In order from oldest to youngest we are: Rachel, Judith, Alexandra, Martha, Ruth, and Caroline.

I had the lucky position of being the first girl, before our parents were actively hoping for another boy. David was always expected to lead the way and do things first, which was sometimes impossible, as he was by nature more cautious. I, on the other hand, could be unafraid to the point of recklessness and loved to show off on the swing set or in any physical activity. That made it easy for me to please my dad. Whenever I charmed Pop with my daring, besides feeling gratified, I always simultaneously could see it from David's perspective: I was showing him up. I loved David and it never pleased me to triumph over him.

Pop was very physical, and loved to play with us when we were young. My favorite time of the day was early morning, especially if I caught Pop before he got out of bed. With my stomach resting on his upraised feet, I held onto his hand and his stub as he lifted me up and flew me all around and over the edge of the bed. I also loved to just talk to him while I watched him shave. In those years our small, modern house had a built-in radio that played in the kitchen and master bedroom simultaneously, so Mother and Pop would be listening to the same program. Part of the program was news, but when Perry Como or Dinah Shore came on, Pop would lift me up and dance me around the room. He would later teach me to waltz and foxtrot.

In junior high, I became interested in sewing and started making many of my own clothes. David often helped me with designs and would sit for hours and talk to me or read to me while I sewed. After the movie *Bonnie and Clyde* came out, I made myself two belted suits like Faye Dunaway's and wore them with long strands of beads or pearls. My mother encouraged me in this activity by paying for as much fabric as I wanted.

I often babysat my younger sisters and for this my parents paid me the grand amount of twenty-five cents an hour, not including the first hour, which I was expected to do for free. At the same time, our allowances were trifling. I never had enough cash and paid for illicit cigarettes with my lunch money. In high school, I wanted to get a job once, but Pop wouldn't hear of it, saying that my only job was to do well in school. I think this was a mistake on his part, but I made the mistake of acquiescing. My younger sisters later got jobs without ever asking permission. After high school, when I went to Wellesley College, I fell back on what I knew and babysat to earn spending money. And I learned more of these lessons the hard way when I left home early, getting married after my first year of college.

Judith was quite small compared to David and me. Pop felt that we could handle it when he bellowed at us and spanked us, but he had to only pretend to give her the same swat because as she stood ready to take it, he lost heart for the whole enterprise. Later, Judith tended to make her way without confronting Pop directly, by simply doing what she intended without a showdown. When we came to Boston University and chose rooms at the president's house on Carlton Street, I picked the big one at the front on the second floor, next to our parents' room. It was quite grand and had its own bathroom. This choice, with such close proximity to our parents' room, led to confrontations whenever I came in late or hadn't picked up my clothes.

Judith chose a room on the third floor at the back, facilitating her coming and going unobtrusively by the back stairs. At school she was a seeker, trying to find her place in the world. She formed a Christian religious study group in high school, and later became an observant Jew. Pop identified with her journey of self-discovery, as he had made a similar one. Religion had been intrinsic to his thinking from an early age. When he went to Yale, it was with the intention of becoming a minister, but he felt liberated when he moved from divinity school to philosophy. Judith's seeking nature led her to earn a law degree as well as a PhD in musicology, and finally to become a history teacher.

Alexandra was born with crazy, curly hair and a fiery temper. When she was still in a high chair, she would cry if you made eye contact with her at breakfast, and she had to have a cereal box placed as a shield in front of her. The year we lived in Germany, we called her "das Baby." She developed a habit of throwing her glass baby bottles out of her crib to see them crash on the floor, and our mother had to write home and ask her mother to find some plastic bottles to send right away. As a sibling, her first instinct was not to bargain, but to fight or tell. I can still hear her yelling at the top of her lungs, "Rachel's smoking in the bathroom!"

What she loved was anything to do with animals, and, for her sake, Pop put up with more pets than he would have ever imagined possible. One little Italian greyhound, named Brutus, particularly had it in for him, leaving surprise offerings on the rug near his bed whenever it got the chance. Alexandra became a vet, which Pop put to full advantage once a year when he took her to Saratoga with a party of his friends and got her to look the horses over before the races. Our dad also valued her medical knowledge and consulted her about our mother's health and his own.

When Mother was pregnant with her next child, she contracted German measles. I thought at the time that we called it German because she caught it in Germany. Our parents were afraid the baby would have Down syndrome and seriously considered seeking an abortion, but decided against it. When Martha was born, perfectly healthy, it was a time of great celebration for our family. I remember the satisfaction and delight we all took in everything Martha did. She was also born with a stalwart, sympathetic nature and she had, and still has, a way of remaining on good terms with all siblings despite a few clashes here and there. She became my little buddy and would sometimes pretend to be my puppy and curl up in my lap or do tricks for me.

Martha reclaimed her Texas roots when she attended college at Trinity, our parents' alma mater in San Antonio, where she majored in business. She seized this opportunity to reinforce ties with all our Texas relatives before returning to the Boston area.

As a wet-behind-the-ears graduate, she landed an accounts receivable job at Lotus in its early days, where she met her husband, Mike. They created a large family of their own with five children, and during those years, Martha gave up her job and did not work outside the home. Martha and Mike helped my parents maintain their property in New Hampshire, which was a source of so much pleasure for the entire family but required a great deal of maintenance as well. My parents also came to rely on Martha as they got older. Martha continues to have a talent for getting along with people, making friends and keeping them, which stands her in good stead not only in her personal life but also in the business world.

When Martha began looking for work after her youngest entered school, she didn't find it easy at first to land a job, but she persevered and took what she could get. She first worked at a less than glamorous job at BJ's, where she refused to give out samples, the first position they offered her, but began instead as a checker and quickly moved up to a job in the office keeping the books. She then moved on to other companies, finally winding up in a terrific position of great responsibility at a financial institution.

After Martha, John and Kathryn didn't plan to have more children, hence the four-year gap before the next one came along. In 1964, at the end of our year in England, Pop remained in Europe with David and me, where he had some work to do at Bonn and then had to drive our new VW bus to Le Havre in order to bring it home with us on the steamship *La France*. While heavily pregnant, Mother took Judith, Alexandra, and Martha home on an earlier ship, the *Sylvania*, from Southampton. Pop would perpetually feel guilty about this arrangement.

When the baby came, Pop, David, and I were still in France, about to board ship, and Kathryn went ahead and named her Laura Ruth, even though she knew that Laura was a name Pop disliked. I always imagine my mother feeling very much like having her own way as she filled in the birth certificate in light of the strenuous journey she had just made to get back to Texas with three young children unassisted. We all knew about the controversy, but Mother won, and we called the baby Laura during the Texas years. However, when we moved to Boston,

Judith convinced Laura Ruth to tell the school that she went by her middle name, Ruth, and the coup in favor of Pop's choice was complete.

Ruth gets her sense of humor from both our parents, but she is also very like Pop physically, in the way she moves. Ruth loves physical activity and became an avid skiing partner for Pop, which was great for him since Mother infinitely preferred to stay at the ski lodge and read. Ruth's athletic interests brought Pop great satisfaction. He gave her a baseball glove and enjoyed going out to the yard and throwing a ball with her.

Ruth's degree is in math, but she also shared Pop's lifelong interest in art. She studied drawing and sculpting at Boston University, and spent some time working in Spain with Sergio Castillo, who created three important works in metals for the Boston University campus. His *Free At Last*, which shows doves taking flight, is dedicated to Martin Luther King's "I Have a Dream" speech and dominates the plaza in front of Marsh Chapel. Castillo's dynamic *Explosion* bursts forth in front of the Metcalf Science Center, and his magnificent *Earth Orbit* maintains an imposing presence in the grand atrium of the Questrom School of Business.

Ruth lived in France for a few years, where her first child was born. When she came back to this country, she first became a high school teacher, then a math professor, and later shifted gears to join a computer software company, working there with younger colleagues, and where I'm sure she fits right in because there is an eternal youthfulness about her.

Caroline was entirely satisfying as the youngest of the family. Her hair curled into natural ringlets and she was very calm and well-behaved, a blessing for older parents. When we arrived in Boston, she was still in nursery school and couldn't even see the tops of the kitchen counters, but she thoughtfully seemed to take in all the activities of the larger folk around her. The fact that, as parents of their youngest daughter, John and Kathryn were on the older side became conspicuous at Caroline's fifth birthday party, during our first year in Brookline. The little guests all seemed to be escorted by their very young, hippie moms.

Caroline developed a strong sense of right and wrong and became very outspoken over perceived unfairness. I noticed this after I married and she and Ruth came to visit me. Our parents had hired a couple to cook and take care of the house. This couple, the Hales, had instituted new rules in the house and the little kids felt insulted and infuriated when they were scolded. Caroline told me all about this with great spirit, her cheeks turning pink with righteous indignation. Caroline earned a master's degree in education, but has made her career in business, her three children being the ones to benefit from her teacher training.

Despite the joys inherent in fathering daughters, Pop often felt outnumbered and had hoped over the years for another son, even talking to Kathryn about possibly adopting a boy. Shortly before we moved to Boston, our neighbors who were close friends died, naming Pop as the guardian of their teenage son. Taking on a fully grown teenager is not the same as raising a baby, and at first the assignment was rather daunting, a culture shock for all sides. Charles drove a race car competitively, and was well-used to doing what he wanted without reference to any authority, and there was more than one run-in with the police. Pop wasn't prepared for these scenarios. Early on, and at his wits' end, he surprisingly counseled Charles to marry his high school girlfriend while they were still in high school, thinking that might help domesticate him. But Charles didn't go for the idea.

After finishing high school in Texas, Charles got rid of the race car and moved in with us in Boston, where he took up karate and went to Boston University. One of the math professors gave his students the assignment of making a graph of all the electrical plugs, light fixtures, and other items where they lived. Charles gleefully turned it into a game, joined in by many of the sisters, racing around the large house, counting and graphing everything. Pop started to appreciate Charles's humor and basic good sense as he got to know Charles better during this period. When another professor was teaching a unit on ecology and suggested that a farmer should refrain from shooting hawks even though they attacked his flocks, Charles responded that that depended on whether the farmer was raising chickens or chicken hawks.

Charles took flying lessons, becoming a licensed pilot, and then worked very hard to learn the math he needed to join the US Air Force as a navigator. He met his wife in the Air Force, a Cuban émigré whose family had fled Cuba and become United States citizens. Pop and Mother hosted their wedding in Florida and flew most of the family down for the festivities. We stayed at a hotel on the beach in Miami and had a big party at Victor's, famous for its Cuban food and music and for the bell out front that the proprietor said would ring only when Cuba was liberated. We toasted the bride and groom and sang "Guantanamera" when the Cuban guitarists performed it.

Conspicuously missing from the festivities was David. I don't remember what excuse he gave for not attending, but he let me know that he could not help feeling Charles's acceptance in the family as a painful slight to himself. Family relations should not devolve to a zero-sum game, but sometimes that's how they feel. This was perhaps inevitable, but nevertheless a sad subtext to this joyous event. Although our parents never legally adopted Charles, he became one of us.

10

David

SOME PEOPLE CAN BE BEST DESCRIBED BY WHAT THEY DO, AND MY brother David did many things beautifully, but his way of looking at the world, his imaginative perspective, was his essence. The year we lived in London, when Pop was on sabbatical from the University of Texas, we went to a London County Council school, their version of public education.

Many kids played soccer, called football, on the playground before school and at every playtime, but David, age eleven, and his best friend would stand on a low wall, less than two feet off the ground, which served as a cliff in their game. Every so often they pretended to fall, stepping off the ledge and spinning in slow motion as if they were tumbling to the rocks below. Then they would laugh and go back to standing on the "cliff."

My brother also became an entertainer during this time and could often be found at recess, surrounded by adoring fellow students, mostly girls, regaling them with stories, songs, bits of dialogue from movies, or whatever came into his head.

One afternoon in November when Pop came out of the Tube station on his way to our nearby home, he was surprised to find David there with a large homemade dummy. David was celebrating Guy Fawkes Day, asking passersby in his acquired English accent, "A penny for the Guy?" Pop did a double-take, hardly recognizing this animated and effusive youngster.

David always preferred to play games that involved acting or inventing stories. For many years, he and Pop had a train set that was ostensibly David's, but he never played with it much by himself. When he did, he was more interested in imagining what was going on in the little stations and villages than watching the engine pull the cars around the tracks.

Acting became more and more the focus of his life, and as soon as he entered high school, he joined Red Dragons, the drama club at Austin High. A few days ago, I watched *The King of Comedy* when it was on television. It isn't Scorsese's greatest work, but it is David's only movie; he mostly acted on the stage. David is just an extra in the film, but, to me, the great thing is that there is a mistake in the continuity. In a scene on the sidewalks of New York, handsome David walks up from behind De Niro and passes him. Then a few seconds later he does it again.

The first house my parents bought in Austin had a large lot that was mostly bare. On weekends, Pop took little four-year-old David with him to the vacant lot at the end of the street where they dug up small trees. At home, where there were already three peach trees at one end of the yard and a loquat bush beside the house, they planted their red bud and sycamore trees, which grew quickly and flourished under their care. Whether learned from these early experiences or innate, David had a magic touch with plants of all kinds.

As an actor, he lived in New York City, in a small rent-controlled apartment. It may have been shabby, but it had stylish old bones and he made it look bohemian and charming. There were always pots of greenery at various stages of growth in all three rooms. One day, he found a plant on the curb that someone had left for the garbage. It looked like a bunch of dead twigs to me, but he cared for it and after a while it sprouted leaves, then flowers, and finally it was covered with tiny oranges. That was David.

With his six younger sisters, David could sometimes be irritable. We girls used to chant "HSN, HSN," for "High Strung Nerves." He had a great sense of style and so we often asked his opinion about our clothes, but his comments were not always flattering. I once asked him how he liked my new blouse and dirndl skirt, to which he replied, "I love it! It looks just like a maid's uniform from an old 1930s movie." Needless to say, my new outfit lost some of its charm.

Another time, my parents were hosting the rehearsal dinner before my wedding. Round tables were set up in the dining room and living room and everything looked beautiful. I came downstairs wearing one of my favorite dresses. It was olive green with subtle pictures of whimsical gorillas and monkeys cavorting on it. Pop took one look at that dress and ordered me to go back upstairs and change. When I furiously told David what had happened, he calmed me, saying, "In the years to come, everyone will be doing this. It will become a traditional marriage ritual where the father of the bride always sends his daughter up to change before the rehearsal dinner, symbolic of the last time he can order her to do anything."

Besides introducing David to horticulture, Pop encouraged his talent as an artist. From a very young age, David had a gift for drawing. While I was busily painting sheets of typing paper with one solid shade from the watercolor box in order to later cut the pages up to make play money, David was drawing and then painting fanciful knights and castles. He was six and we were living in Germany that year while Pop had a Fulbright scholarship to study at Bonn University, beginning his work on Kant. David was enthralled by the many ruined castles, especially die Godesburg and Drachenfels, and the stories that went with them. Pop built an impressive castle out of cardboard with a large, round tower and crenelated walls, perfectly sized to accommodate my brother's set of toy knights. I remember David's concentration as he drew those pictures. His tongue would poke out of the side of his mouth and move infinitesimally, as if it were connected with the clean line appearing on the paper, and his dominant left hand seemed to curl upside down when he drew or wrote. Pop's very large left hand worked the same way, but he said that it wasn't his dominant side; he was left-handed only because he didn't have a right hand.

When we returned to the United States, the mother of the kids next door sent David home because he was drawing pictures of naked women. After spending time in museums on our European travels, he was innocently drawing what he had seen. Pop was impassioned in his defense of David and insulted the lady's small-mindedness while he was at it. One thing our dad never doubted was David's character, and he gave his son a great deal of freedom and responsibility. David got his driver's license at fourteen (the last year it was available at that age in Texas) and he immediately got a car of his own because Grandmother Jewell was ready to let go of her blue Pontiac with chrome fins when she bought a burgundy Grand Prix coupe.

At the same time, Pop must have had some worry about not having introduced David to more manly pursuits. He was much more likely to take his son to a museum, concert, or play than to a ball game. Being so interested in all of the arts himself and not being as much of an enthusiast for team sports, he felt he had let his son down. At one point he asked his friend and graduate student, Bill Bennett, to play football with David. My brother did his best, and he enjoyed hanging out with Bill, but football certainly wasn't going to be his thing. Another time, Pop gave him a copy of *Playboy* magazine, supposedly because of an article he wanted David to read. I have no clue what the "article of interest" was, but the cover had a naked girl dressed up like a Christmas tree. I found the entire issue totally riveting and soon confiscated it from David, who seemed relieved to get it out of his room.

David was always private about his personal life. He had a girlfriend for a time in college and didn't come out openly until later in his thirties, and then, I'm afraid, it was because I had talked with Pop about his being gay, not realizing I was outing him. The thing about a secret is that you have to know it's a secret, or you don't know you're supposed to keep it. I had thought his orientation was obvious by then, but David was livid and took many months to forgive me. Pop's main reaction was pity for David because he would have no children. This was before surrogacy was commonplace. Children were an integral part of Pop's life and he saw the prospect of a childless existence as a bleak landscape.

Pop was never what you could call a homophobe. From what he said privately, it was clear he saw a spectrum of sexuality. As always, he believed foremost in the individual, but he was old-fashioned in that he didn't think one's sexuality was something to discuss publicly. He was especially protective of young people who he felt needed a chance to discover their way for themselves, out of the spotlight. Pop was highly suspicious of encounter-group-style gatherings, seeing them as an invasion of privacy, and he deplored teachers who elicited too much private information in a classroom setting, considering the practice an abuse of power. He believed in protecting the student from classmates who more often than not might be unsympathetic or even cruel.

He was also convinced that young people needed to stay focused on the urgent business of making their way in the world, finding out what they could do well, rather than allowing themselves to be side-tracked too much by sexuality or sex of any kind. I side with Pop in feeling a nostalgia for the lost innocence of bygone eras, and even that of my own generation, when young people had the liberty to form close, affectionate relationships with members of the same sex without making any declarations or denials. The move toward labeling everyone at the earliest age possible in their lives robs them of a great deal of freedom.

Pop subsidized David's income, making it possible for him to pursue a career in acting, despite making very little money at it. He also helped David buy a small country house in New York State, in Columbia County near the Berkshires. It was a retreat for David and a place that was soon blooming with lush vegetation, of both the edible and the decorative variety. By that time he had a partner, Marc, which was a great relief to all of us in the family. We believed the relationship would keep David safe.

11

The *DRAMJACKYL*

Austin, Texas, is surrounded by man-made lakes. Lake Austin runs through the city like a river; in fact it is part of the Colorado River, dammed to maintain a constant level. A perfect heaven for teenagers, it was the lake I was most familiar with because a few friends had motorboats and we liked to ski up and down the lake, stopping sometimes at places where you could pull your boat in and have a hamburger.

The larger lake nearby was Lake Travis. With pleasant inlets and wide dramatic vistas, it was surrounded by hill country, famous for dry brush, cedar trees, and abundant wildflowers. My dad loved Lake Travis and had bought some land overlooking it with the thought that someday he might be able to build a home there. He also had a wider dream that he would elaborate on as we walked the land, a dream of having his children build houses on the property as well, facilitating weekly family meals and the enjoyment of future grandchildren.

Some friends who lived near the lake, Sig and Lys Koch, owned a sailboat that Pop admired greatly. Sig, formerly of the Ford Foundation, had been lured to the University of Texas by my dad. He had a bearded, dramatic face and a way of stammering and gasping and flailing his arms when his speech could not keep up with the brilliant, and often comical, ideas his mind was formulating. Lys was very British and seemed quite formal until you realized she could suddenly, with her most self-possessed, buttoned-down manner, come out with a ribald comment. My dad often went sailing with Sig and learned from him how to navigate the lake.

When Pop felt ready, he bought a boat for us. It was a lovely, twenty-seven-foot beauty with a cabin that had a small kitchen area, a toilet ("the head"), and a bedroom that could have slept two, but we only used it for changing in and out of swimsuits. The first order of business was to name the boat, so I strung together the first initials of my and each of my sibling's names, added in a few extra letters, and came up with the *DRAMJACKYL*, for David, Rachel, Alexandra, Martha, Judith, Caroline, and Laura Ruth. We dedicated the boat at its launch with the old Irish blessing, "May the wind be always at your back and the sun shine on your face," and a bottle of champagne that Pop had cut into so that it would break easily across the bow.

I remember it as an idyllic time. With Pop teaching David to sail, we would tack back and forth across the lake until we came to a pleasant cove where we could drop anchor, go for a swim, and have a delicious spread prepared by my mother that often included guacamole and chips. We also tried nacho cheese Doritos and Bugles for the first time on these excursions, which seemed very new and cool then. Usually it was just the family, but every so often we invited along one or two friends.

Pop said that he had always thought it strange that Homer referred to "the wine-dark sea." He supposed the Greeks must have had some kind of wine that looked bluish or greenish until after looking at Lake Travis under many different conditions and realizing that it sometimes took on shadows that gave it a deep reddish tone. When he noticed the lake darkening with deep ruddy shadows he liked to point it out to us.

Occasionally the weather turned and we would have to return to the marina in the rain. Ever prepared, Pop had all-weather gear stowed aboard. We pulled on the slick, hooded jackets and bounced over the waves as the boat cut toward home. It was exciting to sit right on the bow, holding onto the metal rail when the lake was rough. One time, the wind whipped up so powerfully that the sail tore, but it was only a seam that had come loose and Pop and I were able to sew it back together with zig-zag stitches on the sewing machine.

When we docked the boat, my dad had a meticulous routine. Everything was stowed properly and all surfaces were wiped down. David and Pop dealt with the sails, but everyone helped with the rest. Every crumb and bit of empty packaging had to be thrown away at the marina or brought home. That did not mean, however, that the fun of the day was over. Pop always liked to stop on the way home for ice cream cones, and we would have two scoops, so we could choose two different flavors. One of Pop's would always be chocolate, sometimes both. He always loved chocolate.

One particular day on the lake stands out from the others. My parents and the little kids didn't go along for once and David manned the helm alone for the first time. We took a few friends with us and had a marvelous day. I can still remember the sense of extra joy at being out on the lake without the grownups. We still tacked back and forth across the lake, found a pleasant cove, went for a swim, had a delicious meal, but of course, David and I smoked cigarettes, an expression of our independence. It felt as though a new vista of rewarded responsibility was spreading magnificently before us. All went well, but when we arrived at the marina, there was a message waiting for us. We were to go directly to the Kochs' house nearby and call home.

Sig and Lys let us in, rather grimly it seemed to me compared with the jovial spirits they had always effused before. Judith, Alexandra, and I huddled around David as he made the call, and then told us that Pop had been fired from his job as dean of arts and sciences at the University of Texas. Our parents didn't want us to be shocked if we heard the news on the radio as we drove home. Despite it being very big news in Austin, we weren't exactly disturbed by it. To us it seemed like a thrilling battle, with Pop standing for all that was good, valiant, and true against the apathetic and blind, or perhaps even venal powers that be.

We were well used to him in this role. For as long as we could remember, he had been a leading voice championing urgent causes: against segregation, against capital punishment, and for early childhood education. I remember one time when my parents came to a PTA meeting because I was going to dance and sing on the stage with my class, and the president of the PTA made some sort of inane comment praising the selfless teachers whose dedication to the children was reward enough. I could feel my dad simmering next to me as the poor guy on the stage droned on. Then Pop boiled over, stood up, and gave a rousing speech about the need for higher salaries for teachers, causing the auditorium to go wild with applause. So, we had no doubt that our dad was the knight with pennants flying and Frank Erwin, the chairman of the U.T. Board of Regents, was the dragon. Naturally, when we got in the car, we immediately turned on the radio and hung on every word as a news announcer discussed Pop's firing. And during the following days, we relished every morning newspaper, full of articles and commentary on the subject.

We became well acquainted with the controversy. The board of regents at the university wanted to split up the College of Arts and Sciences into separate colleges, and Pop thought they should stay together because he valued a well-rounded education. He thought future philosophers and historians would be better off, less insular, if they knew something about math and science, and, conversely, he thought that scientists and mathematicians would be better, more enlightened people if they had some experience of the humanities.

This, however, wasn't the only issue involved. Money and politics were root causes as well. The regents were building up the university to the point where it would soon lose the sense of community it enjoyed as a more moderately sized institution. It seemed like the only point of the buildup was to bring in more students to feed the money machine, supporting more businesses and filling more towering, high-rise apartments. The excessive spending on building projects during this era was exemplified by the construction of a house for the U.T. chancellor, the Bauer House, which exuded exaggerated extravagance. A huge mansion with a swimming pool, plus a poolhouse, as well as a guesthouse on the property, were all tucked behind massive ornate gates. We, the older kids, had fun teaching Laura Ruth, at five years of age, to say, "The Bauer House is a monstrosity." It cracked us up every time she said it with her youthful, innocent voice.

There was great excitement in the house the night before Pop went to Corpus Christi to speak at the board of regents meeting. Our dad planned to present the case for a unified College of Arts and Sciences to the board, and perhaps even to get himself reinstated as dean. He and his teaching assistants, Bill Bennett, Bill Burkett, and others, worked all through the night on his speech. The two Bills took turns typing the speech as Pop dictated. The next morning they drove down to Corpus in our station wagon with the two back seats folded down flat so that Pop could stretch out and sleep on the way.

After butting heads with Frank Erwin for some time, JRS wasn't convinced that his opposition to the division of the College of Arts and Sciences, to the ever-increasing student body, and to the seemingly wanton waste of funds would in and of themselves have been enough to cause Erwin to give him the ax. He believed a well-received speech he made at a Houston country club had been the last straw. Frank Erwin could put up with the John Silber who was a liberal firebrand as long as he confined himself to the campus. However, when it appeared that my dad might gain popularity with a wider and well-to-do audience, it would not require a crystal ball to foresee his running for office and dispossessing one of Erwin's chosen candidates.

The year 1970 was a very exciting time, when Pop was receiving offers from universities across the country. At dinner, we would discuss the relative merits of California and Colorado.

The search committee at Boston University, comprised of trustees, faculty, and a few representative students, had considered a wide range of candidates for the position of president and finally narrowed it down to two or three. Melvin B. Miller, the Black publisher and editor of the *Bay State Banner* and a trustee of the university, had an aunt who had been the house mother of the dormitory for Black female students at the University of Texas. U.T. had only recently been forced to desegregate and the innovation did not extend as far as living quarters were concerned until 1969, so this segregated dormitory had been maintained until then. When Mel Miller visited his aunt, she vouched for John Silber, and Mel was then able to forward the information that Silber was a good guy and supporter of liberal causes to the committee. This tipped the scale in Silber's favor. Over the years, Mel Miller has never wavered in his support and continues to be proud of his role in bringing John Silber to Boston University. He and JRS would also bond over their shared heritage, both being part German.

When Pop chose Boston University out of all the positions offered to him, he never looked back. I don't believe he ever had a wistful moment thinking about Texas or anywhere else. He loved Boston from the first and made it our home.

Out in the waters of Martha's Vineyard, Mother and Pop would sometimes sail with Arthur Metcalf, for many years the chairman of the board of trustees at Boston University, and Marcia Hall, his long-time companion, on their beautiful sailboat, the *Veritas*. When Arthur decided to sell his boat, my dad was tremendously excited and made him an offer. A good offer, but Arthur still refused to sell it to Pop, despite the fact that they had become close friends. He believed my dad would not invest the large amount of money needed every year to keep the boat in top condition, which Arthur believed was necessary. He knew Pop well enough to be fairly certain he would scrimp on these expenses, probably trying to do a great deal of the work himself rather than hiring professionals.

Although this was a disappointment, Pop had, in the meantime, bought a small Sunfish sailboat in New Hampshire to tide him over while he was thinking about what kind of larger sailboat to buy. The thing about a Sunfish is that it really holds only two people. As it turned out, Pop particularly enjoyed this kind of sailing with just one other person. It was a chance to have a private conversation with one child, grandchild, or friend, at a time. Pop taught several of his children and grandchildren, including my daughter, Mary Beth, to sail in the crystal clear waters of Squam Lake.

We kept things simple in New Hampshire. Pop had a record player, and a collection of records that he enjoyed playing. Harry Belafonte was a great favorite, and as a wake-up call for late sleepers, Pop liked to play circus music. We had a television but no regular television reception and only used it for movie videos we wanted to watch. All of my kids remember seeing *Blazing Saddles* and *Singin' In the Rain* up at Squam with their grandparents. My mother liked it best when we all played Scrabble.

The first thing Pop did after buying the house on Squam was to remove the dishwasher from the kitchen and replace it with an extra cabinet. All dishes and pans were washed by hand with modest amounts of detergent only after paper towels were used to remove most of the grease from them. He also did not allow us to have a washing machine at the lake house. Any laundry had to be taken into town to the laundromat in order to preserve the purity of the lake as much as possible. This extra work took quite a bit of effort, but we understood Pop's concern. The pristine quality of the water was our responsibility, and he gave it top priority above mere convenience.

One summer, the movie *On Golden Pond* was filmed at Squam Lake. We were always out in the small motorboat putt-putting around the lake, trying to catch a glimpse of Katharine Hepburn. E.M. Heath, the local super market, kept her favorite flavor of Häagen-Dazs in stock for her. We've been trying to remember what flavor it was, perhaps boysenberry. Whenever we went to the store, we kept our eyes peeled for her. Sometimes the stars would land on the lake in a tiny, white seaplane. It looked and sounded like a toy, and we strained our eyes trying to see who it was, but they were too far away for us to tell.

The lake and surrounding mountains couldn't have been more beautiful, and our small house there on Squam was a refuge from the hectic life in the city, a retreat where Pop could write and sculpt, and a holiday haven for my mother, my siblings and me, and all of our children, but I sometimes missed our family sailing trips in the *DRAMJACKYL*, and I don't think I ever saw the crystal clear New Hampshire water turn to wine.

12

Foremost a Teacher

I ALWAYS KNEW MY DAD WAS A TEACHER, THE FRINGE BENEFIT OF this being that he always had paper and pencils we could purloin from his study. We had never been explicitly told not to take them whenever we wished, but David and I used to make sure not to leave the exotic-looking blue box of Venus Velvet pencils empty, and to take only one or two sheets of the typing paper at a time so that the stack didn't change too much.

For chores around the house or yard, Pop always liked having some helpers. On weekends when he cut the grass, each of us was given something to do. We might weed the garden around the green peppers, tomatoes, periwinkles, and marigolds in the beds flanking the front door, or edge the lawn with handheld clippers, which was a big job because the extensive lawn was intersected by brick walks and cement sidewalks. We had several pairs of the clippers so a few of us could work on that.

Pop liked to teach us how to do each job. He didn't just supervise; he was directly involved, putting tremendous energy into each activity, and the outcome really mattered to him. For someone so cerebral, he really liked doing nonverbal tasks. I remember him showing us how to build dikes around the pepper plants to hold some of the water and also teaching me to sweep efficiently so that the dirt and grass didn't go flying at the end of each stroke.

Pop also tried to prepare us for hardship or danger that might come our way. On one of our road trips, Pop had a scare one night as he drove along after everyone else had gone to sleep. As he was driving over a bridge, he saw there was a dark patch ahead. He tried to stop in time, thinking it was a gaping hole, but was relieved when it turned out to be repair work done in dark asphalt. After that, he prepared us in case our car ever went into the water. Sitting around the dinner table, we practiced: wait for the car to settle; team up older kids with younger kids; open the windows and wait for some water to come in; take a deep breath and swim to the surface; meet on the shore.

If we kids squabbled with one another, Pop acted as a judicious arbiter. He was also often amused by our conflicts and the things we said. When I was about two and a half, David, a very mature four-year-old, accused me of lying. Pop intervened and explained to David that I was too young to lie. David thought about it for a moment before replying, "Well then, she's a little liar!"

Whenever we received presents, Pop insisted on us writing thank-you letters. We wrote a rough draft that he would look over and some-times ridicule, especially if it was just a case of laziness and sticking to a formula such as, "Thank you so much for the such-and-such. I really like it. Well, thanks again, Rachel." He might read the unsatisfactory letter back to us in a funny bored voice with a dopey look on his face to get the point of its inanity across and make us laugh.

Pop bought thick leather shoes for us that were designed not for looks but to last for a very long time. The colloquial term for these shoes would be clodhoppers, but we always called them "hodcloppers." He taught us to shine our own shoes, and for a while that was a regular feature of our Saturdays. David, Judith, Alexandra, and I would spread old newspapers on the kitchen floor and go to it with delicious smelling polish. I loved the one called oxblood and liked to use it on my shoes even though they weren't really that color.

Once Pop told us that a friend had caught his daughter stealing money from his wallet, and this father took the cash she had taken and flushed it down the toilet just to show her that it was not the money but the principle that mattered. That impressed me.

Quite often, Pop returned to his office at the University of Texas after dinner to work for a couple of hours, and it terrified us when his car suddenly roared up to the house if he came home earlier than we expected. We'd flip out the lights and hop into bed, but he would sometimes tear up the stairs yelling at us as we tried to pretend we were asleep. A few times on long car trips when we were being rowdy, Pop stopped the car and lined us all up on the side of the road swatting each of us, and giving phony taps to the little ones. I don't remember my mother ever seriously punishing us; however, I do remember her once taking off one of her flip flops and waving it in the air as she chased us. That was when we were very young. She wasn't a disciplinarian, but you would not like to be the object of one of her derisive looks. If she thought you did something stupid, her looks could be quite devastating.

When I was a teenager, during the seventies, I sometimes called Pop "Big Jake," after the John Wayne character, and took it upon myself to try to teach him to be a better parent. He could respond with way too much anger if one of the little kids let a screen door slam after being told not to. One time, Laura Ruth did this on her way out to the side porch where Pop and I were sitting, and he shouted at her each time. I told "Big Jake" he would make a bigger impression on her if he had a talk with her and explained what he wanted. He scoffed a bit, so I called my little sister over and told her clearly what was wanted, and even went over to the door with her and demonstrated how to close it properly, letting her try it a couple of times before she went back into the house. Pop asked, "And that's going to do it?" I responded with assurance. A few minutes later, when Laura Ruth rushed out of the house again, Pop and I both stiffened, expecting the slap of the screen, but she spun around, grabbed the handle, and closed the door just as I had shown her. Pop let me have my victory; he and I just grinned at each other.

In Texas, he had what seemed like hundreds of students. A few of the female students babysat us on occasion, but we got to see them all at the big party my parents had for them at the end of each year. These were joyous parties with masses of Mexican food from El Toro, a local restaurant. The students were always very exuberant, running all around the house and yard, and Pop was in his element, joking and laughing with them.

One of his big assignments each year was called "The Slum Project." Pop sent the students out to find an area that was run down with urban blight and then to look into the background of that piece of property. They were to interview the tenants. Find out who the owner was. Was it an absentee landlord? Were the owners fulfilling their legal obligations to their tenants? This was serious work for undergraduate kids, but they seemed to like it and were proud of what they were able to discover. One year, as a prank, a group of students put together a slum project packet on our home, with a photo of our house on the cover. Pop treasured this humorous effort for years to come.

When JRS first arrived at the University of Texas, he was not much older than his students. He told me that he found a few of them to be rather more experienced in some ways than he was. One of the most worldly was George Krimpas, a handsome, flamboyant young man from Greece. He would later become involved in economic policy in his country. On our family's first trip to Europe, in 1959, we stayed with him in London for a few days, where he cooked a delicious egg concoction for our breakfast that he called "'am and heggs," having fun with the British penchant for dropping or adding their h's. This dish made with ham, eggs, tomatoes, and parmesan became a regular fancy breakfast in our family.

The next time we saw George Krimpas was when he came to stay for several days in 1964, the year we lived in London. He was full of fun and his excitement was infectious. He brought us a record of Greek music and taught us to dance in a line, snaking uproariously through our flat. Many years later, Judith and Martha traveled with Pop to Greece, where they delighted in their joyous reunion with George Krimpas and his family. He was still as high-energy and fun as ever.

Willie and Celia Morris were a particularly sophisticated couple among Pop's early students. They drank hard liquor for one thing. Willie was editor of the *Daily Texan* his senior year and would go on to edit the *Texas Observer* and then *Harper's Magazine*. He also would write *North Toward Home* among other titles. Celia wrote several books as well. We later visited them as a family on our trips across country, and during Pop's sabbatical in 1960, we spent time with Celia on a visit to Paris, where she recommended the best things to order at charming little sidewalk restaurants. I wasn't too impressed by the spinach purée she vouched for, but my parents thought it was fantastic and Pop insisted I eat several bites of it. Mother helped by hiding the spinach on my fork under a delicious slice of steak.

One student Pop became very fond of despite their frequent arguments was Mike Gordy, a full-fledged Marxist. Gordy would later move to France, where he went into the business of marketing wines.

My parents frequently visited him and his family on their trips to Europe.

Over the years, JRS kept up with a number of students in person or through correspondence, and whenever visiting U.T. to make speeches or attend events, he was delighted to reconnect with more of them.

He always had a few candidates for PhDs. They were well acquainted with his teaching style because they also acted as his teaching assistants and attended his lectures. Some of them told us that one time, when he was lecturing about the difference between right and power, one of the students, acting cocky, said he didn't get it. According to legend, Pop rushed over to the student, pushed him down on the floor and shoved his stub up under the kid's chin. From that vantage point he asked the boy, "Now I have the power to do you some harm, but you have to tell me, do I have the right?"

Many of his graduate students became longstanding friends of our family. Ed Delattre, who used to teach us magic tricks, became a dean of the Boston University School of Education for a time and then went on to become the president of St. John's College. An expert in police protocol, he wrote a book on law enforcement ethics. He and his wife Alice would continue to visit Pop at least once a year.

One of the most lively graduate students was Terry Pinkard, who babysat us sometimes when my parents went on trips. He taught David and me some rock and roll songs. I remember us dancing around the kitchen with him, singing "Runaround Sue," and I imagine he is never dull as a professor.

Bill Bennett became well-known for *The Book of Virtues*, as secretary of education under Ronald Reagan, and as drug czar under George H. W. Bush. I remember Pop sold him an old heap of a used car we called "The Big Bubble." In Texas, Pop was always on the lookout for secondhand cars. He would buy them inexpensively, fix them up, and sell them to visiting professors and graduate students who often needed something reliable when they got to town.

For a while we owned a big black Cadillac limousine that Pop bought cheaply from a funeral home. I'm proud to say that my parents were both brave enough to drive this showy car around town with all of us kids luxuriating in the back, playing with the electric switch that put the window up or down between the front and back seat. Some would have been embarrassed to indulge in this kind of fun.

The car Pop sold to Bill Bennett looked like something a movie gangster or a Humphrey Bogart-style private eye would drive. Although the TAs seemed very grown up to my siblings and me (one even smoked a pipe), they were really still just kids. At Pop's student party one year, Bill brought his electric guitar. He played it after dinner out on the lawn, off the side patio under the spreading branches of the pecan tree, until the police came and asked him to stop.

This may have been the same year that David did an impersonation of Pop teaching. David stuck his right hand up under his armpit and walked around gesticulating alternately with his left hand and his pretend stub. He had gotten the idea from a film of Pop teaching, made for a program called "Meet the Professor." Pop had brought the film home and set it up on a projector in the living room for us to see, but the subject matter was too difficult for me to understand at that time.

Years later, I was lucky to be there when Pop taught a class as a presentation for a group of educators at a university. It must have been for a college of education because the audience included several high school teachers who had each brought a number of select students, chosen to be the "classroom" for him to teach.

Pop took Judith, Alexandra, and me along so that we could observe him in action. For us, as high school students ourselves, it was exciting to be spending time on a college campus. We even had a room to share in a dormitory. We were just a few doors down a corridor from an open living room area by the elevators where cool-looking college kids were hanging out. Our dad had given us some reading to do in our dorm room to prepare for the class, but we were mostly just chatting and looking out the window.

Pop came by once to check on how we were getting along. When he knocked, we asked, "Who's there?" And he answered in his comical, mock-serious, deep voice, "It is I." After he left, the college boys who had overheard kept amusing us by knocking on our door and saying, in deep bass voices, "It is I."

The class Pop taught was supposed to demonstrate the use of the Socratic method in the classroom. He introduced this to the students and explained briefly how it worked. He said he would be asking the class questions, and that the students should think seriously and give thoughtful answers. The students were also to come up with questions of their own that would further the discussion.

This day's subject was abortion. He led the high school students to think deeply and express themselves on this delicate subject by asking question after probing question. I remember very clearly the part of the discussion where the class was trying to decide: What is the fetus? Besides a blackboard, Pop didn't have any visual aids, but with just words he asked the class to consider what the fetus looked like at different stages, and what might be going on with the developing heart, brain, fingertips. He asked, "Could this be a developing baby elephant?" Of course, the students laughed.

Eventually, the class came to the conclusion that the fetus had to be a human being. Then began the consideration of whether or not it was all right to terminate that life. After many questions and much discussion the class came to the tentative conclusion that as a human being it should have some rights, but in some cases it would be reasonable to end this human life, in a way similar to justifiable homicide. Nobody's arm was twisted. The students came to these determinations by answering questions and thinking seriously about the subject. From Pop's point of view, the purpose was to make the students think. There was no right or wrong answer; it was open ended. I don't think my dad *ever* felt like he had entirely finished thinking about this topic.

In any event, at this point there was a break. Everyone went out in the hall for a much-needed intermission and the students regrouped with their own teachers. When the class reconvened it was obvious that the thought police was in force, even back in the 1970s. The teachers were more interested in teaching their students what to think rather than how to think. During the recess they had whipped their students back into shape. The young people no longer answered freely but instead made broad statements that had no basis in the antecedent questions or discussion. These were mere slogans that were meant to stop the discussion as if these matters were already decided and did not need to be discussed.

The teachers had laid down the law to maintain the status quo, and their best and brightest students, who relied on them for their grades, kowtowed. Pop was bitterly disappointed by the way things went, but I was proud of him that day, and Socrates would have been, too.

13

A True Liberal

Why was John Silber considered liberal in Texas but conservative at Boston University? The brusque, confrontational manner with which he approached the red ink and other difficulties of the job in Boston probably contributed to the discrepancy. At the same time, he was essentially the same man. His views on many liberal issues had not changed; he continued to support equal rights, affirmative action, early childhood programs for nutrition and education, and he still opposed capital punishment.

John Silber addressed this inconsistency himself in an article he wrote for the *New Criterion*, "Procedure or Dogma: The Core of Liberalism." This essay is also a chapter in his 2013 book, *Seeking the North Star*. The *New Criterion* recently reprinted it, and the essay is as informative for today's world as it was when originally printed in 1999. I will quote from it frequently in this chapter to elaborate on this subject in my dad's own words.

In "Procedure or Dogma: The Core of Liberalism," JRS relates cathartic moments in his journey of self-discovery as a liberal. In one of the earliest, as a ten-year-old, he rose to give his seat on a bus to a Black woman he "perceived to be elderly." Young Johnny was doing what he had been taught to do by his parents, but others on the bus shouted at him to sit down and called him a "nigger-lover." The woman passed by and went to the back of the bus, but my dad "remained standing…furious at the violation of everything I had been taught in Sunday School." As he recalled it in his essay, "I think it was the first indication that I was a liberal."

During the Depression, my dad's father, Paul G., continued to be "a staunch Republican, remembering better times under Hoover" even though he was beginning to get work thanks to "the ripple effect of modest recovery" created by Roosevelt's building programs. After living in one rented house after another, Pop's mother, Jewell, had bought a small house for the family, paying only $25 down. Then, when Paul G. "received approval of a loan from the Home Owners' Loan Corporation, one of Roosevelt's New Deal initiatives" to realize his dream of enlarging it and "making it livable," Johnny asked his father, "Why are you against Roosevelt? Everything good that has happened to us has happened under Roosevelt." That was when my dad realized he was a Democrat.

He also remembered that when a student swing band became so popular that it was hired to perform at big dances in place of professionals, the high school music director "arranged for them to join the Musicians' Union without paying the initiation fee on condition that from that time forward they would charge union scale." The music director "explained that when high school kids without families to support charged less than half union scale, they took bread out of the mouths of the families of adult musicians." The lesson was clear to my dad. As he put it, "This seemed right to me: I continued to be a liberal."

Each experience taught him something new about doing what he thought was right, which he equated with being a liberal. At the University of Texas in 1957, he put his job on the line to support Barbara Smith, a Black student who "was thrown out of the School of Music's production of Purcell's *Dido and Aeneas* on orders from the administration. The only objection to Miss Smith was that she was Black." When legislators objected and "anonymous callers...threatened violence," university officials gave in to these pressures. As Pop was to learn, he could not count on other so-called liberals to stand with him. "Despite the fact that Miss Smith's moral and legal rights were being violated, a committee of senior faculty, including Dean Page Keeton of the law school and other eminent 'liberals,' found that no reasonable person could disagree with the decision of the Chancellor. I observed then, and have never forgotten, that persons recognized as liberals sometimes behave as if they were autoimmune diseases designed to attack their own kind."

For my dad, being a liberal was related to being a philosopher. The method of questioning what is right and true as a liberal is similar to Socratic dialectic and to the scientific method. It is a search for the best possible answer with the available information. As he saw it, a liberal looks at all sides of an issue and listens to all voices, considering all points of view. That is why freedom of speech is so fundamental and vital. As a liberal, your point of view is never fixed in stone because you are always ready to hear from a new voice, a different perspective. As he put it, "We never reach the truth, only the likeliest account, which may require revision or even rejection on the basis of subsequent evidence and argument."

JRS suggested that some positions might seem fixed because "some facts never change and some arguments are not refuted." However, he determined that "one is not a liberal but an ideologue if one joins the thought police to enforce political correctness in society and especially in academe."

In *Seeking the North Star*, JRS added an introduction that was very helpful in positioning the controversy:

> In 1999, the *New Criterion* devoted an issue to the study of liberalism and invited me to contribute. The editor, Roger Kimball, was highly critical of John Stuart Mill and liberalism as he presented it. It was my opinion, however, that Kimball's objection was not to Mill, but to the current confusion of liberalism with left-wing views. I wrote this essay to make clear that one cannot define liberalism as holding left-wing positions—or conservatism as holding to right-wing positions. Liberalism is more accurately defined not as a position but as a procedure by which ideology is avoided through a principled search for truth.

Protecting freedom of speech from the attacks of those who tried to disrupt and prevent it at Boston University was often challenging:

> Our administration kept an open campus to ensure the exercise of First Amendment rights and the right of free assembly no matter how hard activist faculty and students tried to shut it down. One eminent and thoughtful captain of the Thought Police was Howard Zinn. When our Latin-American development center organized an international conference attended by, among others, Presidents Eduardo Frei of Chile and Carlos Lleras Restropo

of Colombia, Zinn attempted with the help of his students to disrupt it. The police had to be called to restore order and remove the disrupters. It was however, a civilized use of force to preserve academic freedom and our rights to free speech and assembly. The Zinn principle could be summed up as holding that all academics were entitled to academic freedom, but that some academics were not.

The example of Howard Zinn shows how far we have come from the liberal ideal practiced by Socrates and developed by Milton and Mill. Socrates taught us to prize those persons of knowledge, candor, and good will who challenge our views, and to be especially grateful when we are shown to be mistaken. For then we exchange a false opinion for a truer one.

Sadly, we seem to be moving ever farther from the liberal ideal on college campuses today with violent protests and attacks, mostly on conservative speakers, denying them the right to speak and be heard, at an all-time high.

My dad found that there was a litany of left-wing beliefs that one was expected to hold in order to be considered a liberal. He demurred from this notion, explaining that "a liberal defends and sometimes exercises the right to be politically incorrect in the Socratic and Millian pursuit of the truest account. Whether evidence or argument leads him to the left or right, he remains a liberal and has every right to object when he is pejoratively described as a conservative."

He held it to be unfair to use adherence to any particular belief to determine whether one was a liberal or conservative. As he affirmed, "Whenever one uses a set of beliefs as a liberal litmus test, one has confused liberalism with dogmatism." And he continued, "the ideologue of the left is no more liberal than the ideologue of the right, for neither believes in humility before the facts and logic, respect for the experience and views of others, and the importance of making a supreme effort to avoid irrationality."

JRS questioned those who claim to be liberal despite their illiberal thinking and found fault with both liberals and conservatives whose way of thinking begins with a conclusion and then sifts through examples looking only for evidence supporting that view:

> Many today who wear their liberalism on their sleeves are far from liberal. The rigidity of their adherence to dogmas exposes them as ideologues. And their use of "conservative" as a pejorative epithet is without justification. Many conservatives adhere to the liberal procedure of inquiry but, while following evidence and argument, arrive at conclusions that are right-wing. But there are also ideologues on the right who use evidence and argument to support only antecedent conclusions. They are more accurately described as dogmatic reactionaries.

JRS denigrated ideologues of any stripe that refuse to put their beliefs to the test of dialogue and argument.

My dad was first introduced to the Boston University search committee by a Marxist professor, Robert Cohen, whom he had known at Yale when they were fellow graduate students. The famous firing of John Silber at U.T. and the news stories enumerating his many left-wing views, led Cohen and other Marxists on the committee to believe my dad was sympathetic to their agenda. This belief couldn't last. As my dad put it, "Ideologues, as the Marxists were, do not listen carefully; otherwise, they could never have been confused about my position. Within months, however, the truth began to out, as bit by bit I was incrementally exposed as a liberal, or to use their term of art, a fascist."

Despite the hyperbolic name-calling he sustained, the only sense in which my dad conceded that he was conservative was "in the sense that we conserve a methodology begun by Socrates and essential to all scientific thought. But since this mode of thought was systematically presented by Mill, those of us who follow that method are justified in calling ourselves liberals and may expect to be recognized as such. The procedure defines the essence of liberalism." As a true liberal, my dad shunned dogma and upheld the great tradition of enlightened thinking.

14

The House on Carlton Street

WHEN WE FIRST CAME TO BOSTON, THE UNIVERSITY HAD TO ACQUIRE a new president's house for us. In Father Marsh's day, the president and his family had lived at the heart of the campus in a house with Gothic details on Bay State Road called "The Castle," but the upper rooms had been turned into offices since then. Arland Christ-Janer, the president before John Silber, was too afraid of student unrest to live anywhere near campus, so the university had bought a house in Wellesley for him to live in, well away from possibly unruly students.

When our family first walked through the house on Carlton Street, just across a Massachusetts Turnpike overpass bridge from the university, it seemed very dark and gloomy. Unlived in for a long time, the walls and floors were covered in dust and the electricity wasn't even connected. The kitchen still had a large old stove that burned wood rather than using gas or electricity, and the basement had a drying chamber with racks for drying clothes. Pop let my siblings and me choose our rooms, and then for several months we went to live in a house nearby that belonged to the parents of Hans Estin, the chairman of the board of trustees of Boston University at the time.

It is hard to believe how different New England seemed from anything we had been used to. Back then, in the 1970s, places were more culturally isolated than they are now. The first time Mother bought a cut-up chicken from our nearby store, the Beacon Supermarket, she found that it was cut so that there was no wishbone piece. Every piece counts when you have a large family, and besides, the kids, including Pop, loved the pulley bone for making wishes. Mother asked the butcher at the Beacon Supermarket if he could cut the next chicken the way she wanted it, and he invited her back behind the counter to show him how to do it. This was the beginning of a long and satisfying relationship between my mother and this grocery store.

Despite being called a supermarket, it was really a very small space and didn't carry every brand. The owners chose the ones they thought were best or the ones requested by their customers. They had mostly Cott (*It's Cott to be good!*) soda, a local brand we had never heard of, rather than Coke and Pepsi. We were surprised to find that the kids at school called it "tonic." It was impossible to find Big Red or ingredients for Mexican meals, and we would ask friends and family flying in from Texas to bring the distinctive red soda, tortillas, and Ro-Tel tomatoes. Pop introduced us to Bailey's ice cream sundaes, one of his most exciting discoveries, served with their delicious hot fudge spilling over the edge of a silver dish onto a silver plate. I felt like I became acquainted with the area by learning how to get to one Bailey's location or another.

In those early days, the whole family used to just pile into the station wagon and drive around, getting our bearings and seeing the sights. We were told that Boston was called "The Hub," as in "the Hub of the Universe." In our initial jaunts around town, I got the impression that the hub of Boston was Kenmore Square. Then, in the 1970s, it was not only dominated by the Citgo sign with its distinctive neon pyramid; it also had a gorgeous White Fuel sign, with sparkly gold neon bubbling up out of an oil derrick and cascading down in streams of shimmering white light to spell *White Fuel.*

Commonwealth Avenue and Beacon Street crossed one another there, at Kenmore. Going east, these two streets led to the Back Bay and downtown Boston where there was a Bailey's, and going west, they led through the main campus of Boston University and into Brookline. Brookline Avenue emanated from Kenmore in a western direction as well, leading past Fenway Park and connecting to Boylston Street, which led to the Bailey's in Chestnut Hill. Pop had originally introduced us to both this Bailey's and the one downtown, but David and I took over the Chestnut Hill location as one of our late-night haunts, a place to go for coffee and cigarettes, back when you could still smoke indoors and coffee was served in real crockery cups rather than paper.

When we finally moved into the house on Carlton Street, it had been beautifully restored. The walls on the first floor were covered with silk damask and the dark mahogany cabinets, buffet, and sliding doors of the dining room and living room were newly stained and polished. We children were pleased with the wallpaper or paint we had chosen for our own bedrooms and the large playroom on the third floor had fun blue covered foam cushions, designed by Roberto Matta in 1966, that could fit together like a puzzle or could be used singly as chairs and lounges. The only things that didn't seem quite right were the columns in the front entryway. They had been painted to look like marble, but they really just looked like wood that was dabbed with various shades of paint.

We enjoyed getting used to the high-powered telephone system in the Carlton Street house. There were three telephone lines, one for personal family use, one for the university, and surprise of surprises, one for the children that didn't even ring in our parents' bedroom! In Texas, we had had one telephone line and only one or two telephones on each floor of the house. Pop had installed a buzzer in the wall on each floor, and the idea was that we wouldn't have to yell up the stairs to get someone to answer the phone. If you wanted someone to pick up on the third floor, you pressed the buzzer three times. If you wanted someone to pick up on the second floor, you pressed twice. An extended buzz meant it was dinnertime. The phones at Carlton Street were much snazzier. First of all, each room had a phone, even the little kids' rooms. Each phone had a designated number, and the intercom on that phone could be called by dialing that number.

There was also an antique intercom system in the house, and the beautiful brass instruments were built into the wall in several locations with buttons to press for every other location. Each brass set had a black cone-shaped spout you could talk into, and attached to the set by a wire was a round black ear phone hanging from a hook that you could lift and hold to your ear. We children figured out which of the antique intercoms still worked and loved using them as a game, even though some of the cloth-covered wires were threadbare and looked like they would electrocute you if you touched them. We did get a shock now and then.

A large house like that needs a great deal of maintenance, and in addition to the maids who came daily, the search was on for a husband

and wife to live in and keep house. This was quite a change from our household arrangements in Austin where a very sweet woman, Mrs. Paula, came in five days a week to clean and do laundry. Her husband was a groundskeeper at the University of Texas, and the couple sometimes came to stay when our parents traveled. Mrs. Paula liked to bake dozens of yellow cupcakes with pink icing when she took care of us. We didn't really like the cupcakes, but we didn't want to hurt her feelings, so one time we flushed them down the toilet, sadly causing it to stop up, revealing what we'd done.

The maid before her was a with-it Black woman named Freddie. The first thing she would do when she arrived each morning was to ask, "Where's your daddy's little black radio?" The way she said it seemed to emphasize and approve of the fact that it was black, and she would take it with her around the house, changing the station from whatever Pop had chosen to something more hip with Aretha Franklin and Marvin Gaye.

Suddenly trying to do everything on a larger scale and in a higher style in Boston was not easy. The first couple my mother hired didn't want to live in the house. Perhaps Kathryn chose them because she preferred that arrangement as well, being unused to having strangers in the house twenty-four hours a day. They were from Spain and had very elegant manners. The trouble was that they were so refined that Mother felt hesitant about asking them to do any housework, even though they were very amenable and tried to do whatever was needed. They obviously had never done this kind of work before. The one thing they did perfectly was to make a lovely paella.

After the elegant Spaniards, there came a British man and wife named Stanley and Ann, whom we kids called "Stanley and Annley." They also weren't able to manage the work but were minus the charm. Then came another British pair called the Hales. John and Kathryn found they could work with this couple. Our dad appreciated Mr. Hale's dedication to the job. Educated in some other field, he found the work of running a large household more pleasing. Mr. Hale and my dad would keep up a correspondence long after the job ended. Julia Child visited once and the Hales created a special veal dish in her honor. When my mother explained that they had invented the dish for the occasion, Julia couldn't have been more lovely, coming into the kitchen to praise the meal.

As it turned out, President Christ-Janer had not been entirely ridiculous in fearing to live in close proximity to the campus. Protests against the draft and the war in Vietnam on college campuses in the United States were ignited further by our military involvement spreading into Cambodia in the early 1970s. Students held marches and demonstrations, sometimes becoming violent, throwing firebombs and setting fires on campuses, especially to R.O.T.C. buildings.

I attended one such demonstration as a high school student on the University of Texas campus in Austin before our move to Boston. We wore black arm bands to commemorate the lives of the many young soldiers already lost in the war. It was frightening when the marching students reacted in a rush, as a crushing herd, when tear gas was sprayed by the police. But fleeing the police in a stampede of young protesters was not nearly as frightening as being the focus of an angry mob.

One night when Pop was out of town, the students rioted in the street in front of the house. It was terrifying for all of us, especially since our dad wasn't there. The students shouted angrily and even burned Pop in effigy.

It may seem like boisterous fun to the students who are protesting, but it is very scary seeing a crowd of snarling humanity setting fire to a dummy with one short arm that is supposed to be your father. My mother took the little kids to the hallway where there were no windows in case of Molotov cocktails. The older kids were watching the action from my bedroom windows on the second floor. David said it must be what the French Revolution had been like.

The next day a box of elegant chocolates arrived in the mail. There was no card enclosed and we had no idea who it was from. We thought it might be poisoned, a new plot concocted by the crowd that hated us, so none of us would eat any of the delicious-looking confections until we learned later that it was from Pop who was away giving a talk in San Francisco.

If Pop had been at home, the riot on Carlton Street would have been an entirely different experience. Pop seemed to relish confrontations with students. He would have gone out and spoken to them and probably shamed them for trying to scare his kids. He was always ready to communicate, and he kept it in perspective. These were students, somebody's children, and this was a chance for them to learn something.

There were times when the police had to be called in to protect people and property, but Pop was always aware that the goal was to curb violence and bring an opportunity for debate. He was appalled by the outcome at Kent State where four students were killed by the gunfire of nervous National Guardsmen. At the time he said disgustedly, "There are a lot of ways you can deal with kids without shooting them."

After Christmas, a few months after we moved into the house on Carlton Street, we drove to Vermont for a skiing vacation. Mammy was visiting and planned to stay behind with the little kids who didn't ski yet. At the last minute, my parents decided they should go too, so we all made the trip. While we were away, someone set fire to the house. It began in the basement and burned up through the living room and dining room on the first floor, my parents' room and Pop's study on the second, and up through two bedrooms on the third floor.

Mary Jane Hemperley, the vice president in charge of the budget and a close family friend, had not heard about our change of plans and thought that the little kids and Kathryn's mother were still inside. She frantically implored the firemen, "Find the babies! Find the babies!" The firefighters searched the burning house until someone was able to get Pop on the phone and found out we were all safe.

We came back to a charred, smoky mess. So much was lost. Many of our possessions were destroyed. My parents lost all of their clothes, as the fire tore right through their walk-in closet. They had to buy bare necessities right away. Many family photos were gone. The books on the shelf in my room were not entirely burned but had suffered from the intense heat, smelled of smoke, and were browned and curled around the edges. The whole house was infused with smoke as were all our remaining clothes and belongings. Worst of all, Pop's manuscript pages and notes for his great work on Kant were burned. Only bits of the pages were recoverable and only years later would he get back to the project and begin again, rewriting the lost material.

Once again we had to move into another house in Brookline while the house on Carlton Street was restored. The police and fire department proved it was arson, but never discovered who set the fire in our basement. During this time, Pop was also receiving threats on his life, and police were assigned for our protection. They drove us to school and kept an officer on duty around the clock at our rented house. One night a man with a gun got onto the property and climbed onto the flat roof of the garage, near to the kitchen windows, but he was stopped there and didn't get any farther.

After many months, we moved back to Carlton Street. Some things were restored to perfection. Others could not be fixed or replaced. There was a telltale difference in the shade of the smoke-darkened damask on the walls by the curving front stairway and the section of it that had burned and been replaced with new fabric. The only things that had actually been improved were the two columns in the front entryway that were painted with many colored dabs of paint. The smoke and heat had tempered the paint, giving it a smoky patina that did, as if by magic, make the columns look like real marble.

15

High Life

Everything was on a grander scale when we arrived in Boston. The city was larger than Austin, and driving was an insane racecourse with other drivers refusing to give way when you tried to change lanes. I got my license just before the move, and getting on the road was still an exciting adventure. Mother would pay me a dollar a ride to drive her to difficult to reach places like the airport or downtown. I thought, "Oh, I'm so much more adventurous than she is." It seemed clear to me that my mother was intimidated by Storrow Drive and the Callahan Tunnel while I enjoyed driving there. But I later realized she wasn't afraid of driving herself, she just wanted to make sure I had more supervised practice.

The first big event we attended as a family was the commencement at which Pop was inaugurated as president of Boston University. His speech, "The Pollution of Time," was an astute address on the loss of connection between the young and the old. This was a great day for our family, the beginning of our new life. Pop never, ever called Boston University "B.U.," and he once corrected me when I said it. The name was always given the utmost respect by him, a signal of the reverence in which he held his opportunity.

The large party after that first commencement ceremony, at the George Sherman Union, seemed very institutional. The food was not delicious and the attempts at elegance were on the level of using lots of paper doilies and hollowing out lemons or oranges as receptacles for sauces. The first university parties at the Carlton Street house were similarly uninspired.

Pop valued the social side of life and liked to become better acquainted with his colleagues. To this end, he had always felt it was beneficial to regularly get together with fellow professors and their spouses in a convivial way. In the early days at the University of Texas, my parents often had parties for the philosophy department, even before he became its chairman. He remembered that before their first little university party, he looked up the recipe for sauce Louis in *The Joy of Cooking* and made it as a dip for canned smoked oysters. This became a staple of their early Texas parties. Some of the dip, with little puddles of oil from the oysters, would be left over in the morning, and before our parents were up, we children would stir toothpicks around in the dish, then lick the pungent sauce and savor its smoky richness, pretending to be partygoers.

As a fledgling professor, John didn't always remember his party manners at those early collegiate get-togethers. I can remember my mother's scathing looks and comments after a few occasions when he had gotten out of line by being way too argumentative. She would have preferred him to present his more charming side all the time, but as that was not possible, she was at least, with some derision, able to convince him that even occasionally devolving into a heated debate was not suitable for what were supposed to be genial affairs.

The parties in Austin became larger and more sophisticated as JRS became the chairman of the Philosophy Department and then the dean of the College of Arts and Sciences. For these, my parents hired a bartender to handle the drinks, but Mother still did most of the cooking, and my parents maintained the guiding principles of quality and simplicity.

He and his most intimate friends among the faculty at the University of Texas formed a club, called The Arts and Darts Club. They met once a month for darts, which Pop had come to enjoy during our year in London, but mainly they got together to talk and make each other laugh.

Entertaining at Boston University advanced rapidly toward my parents' taste with new management in the evolving food service. Simplifying the décor and upping the quality led to something more elegant. Pop loved planning parties and was fastidious in devising every feature. He ordained that flower arrangements must be low to the table to facilitate talking across them, and my parents carefully orchestrated the seating plans, positioning and repositioning the names until they were satisfied.

Mother liked some of it, especially planning menus, and they both enjoyed working with all the people who made these festivities possible, from planning to presentation: the many heads of food service, florists and furniture movers, as well as cooks and servers. Pop had a special fondness for Rose Girouard, a longtime waitress at every event. Sometimes she would stand at attention as he pretended to be a commanding general inspecting his troops. When doing this, they were like kids together, and they both seemed to get a particular kick out of their game.

Rose, who still works at the university, told me recently that my dad really trained her to do the job the way he wanted it done, but that he made it fun and she never realized he was doing it at the time. She also remembered his playful side. Once when she was opening the door for guests as they arrived at the Carlton Street house, Pop came to tell her that the only remaining guest would be quite late. Rose replied that she didn't mind waiting by the door until the last guest arrived. Pop responded, giving her an exaggeratedly pathetic look and saying, "But then who will take care of me?" After telling me this story, Rose turned to me wistfully, and said, "There isn't a day when I don't miss John Silber."

Rose and another waitress, Marie, became friendly with all of us kids, as well. For a span of years, some of the events turned out to be weddings, as all of the daughters got married, some more than once. Pop paid for these receptions himself, but they took place at the George Sherman Union, the Castle, the Fuller Building, or the Carlton Street house or garden.

The ultimate event every year was the commencement celebration. The party was no longer held in the student union, except when necessary for security reasons, as in the year that Presidents George H. W. Bush and François Mitterrand attended. Usually it was held in the yard where a tent was erected for the huge party. Besides the commencement speaker, who might be a world leader, author, artist, philanthropist, or individual with some other special gift to be honored, there were always members of the manifold university community, as well as other artists, politicians, business leaders, and thinkers of all kinds. My parents were truly up to the mark for these gatherings, not just there to pass the time of day spouting pleasant greetings and party fluff. They were prepared, aware of ideas and issues of the day, and they would have read their guests' books or articles, seen their plays and movies, listened to their concerts or CDs, followed their strategic planning for local, national, or world affairs. This was a social gathering but still on the continuum of our parents' intellectual life.

One year Tom Wolfe made the commencement speech and received an honorary degree. Wolfe, who was famous for always wearing elegant white suits, was nevertheless attired in a traditional black cap and gown for the graduation. Pop surprised him during the ceremony by having a specially made white cap and gown trimmed in Boston University scarlet velvet slipped over his head, on stage in the middle of the ceremony, to his delight. His recent novel at that time, *A Man in Full*, was a favorite of both my parents and one of the few books they both recommended to me. Pop even let me borrow his highly annotated copy. I never asked my dad about it, but I did wonder if he identified with the young man in the book who had an extraordinarily large hand, developed that way from hard labor. It certainly called to my mind Pop's overly developed left hand, which Pop thought had grown that way from overworking it as the other one was missing. I also wondered if Tom Wolfe had gotten the idea for this feature of his character from my dad's hand.

Life at the university, and in a community like Boston, lends itself to this sort of society. Pop's staff prepared my parents with information about new people they would meet. Also, Leonard Kopelman of the Boston Consular Corps often helped facilitate the visits of foreign dignitaries. One time, King Hussein of Jordan visited with his wife, Queen Noor, and some of his adult children. It had been originally thought that their younger children might attend, so my parents asked my husband and me to bring our children as well. I felt especially fortunate to meet these charming people. There was a very strong sense of how tight the security was for that visit, with several bodyguards hiding high-powered weapons under their trenchcoats, hovering and mingling among the guests. The one who sat at our table looked like the actress Debra Winger playing the part of a humorless, vigilant secret agent.

My six-year-old son, James, didn't own a suit at the time. We got the invitation at the last minute, and there wasn't time to buy one, so he wore his jacket of faux white leather with race car names on it. It turned out that King Hussein was a race car enthusiast, and he enjoyed telling James about the brands and races represented there. James hadn't quite caught the king's name accurately, and he later referred to him with a title that sounded straight out of a fairytale: The King Who Sang.

Another time, my parents were invited by Queen Elizabeth II and Prince Philip to a party on the yacht *Britannia* when it was docked in Boston. After that meeting, Pop felt a special regard for Queen Elizabeth, whose probity and intelligence he admired and who was his contemporary, both having birthdays in 1926. Mother, on the other hand, was especially taken with Prince Philip for his unorthodox charm and wit.

For smaller dinner parties, Mother and the Hales handled everything, but for the many kinds of larger parties at the Carlton Street house, the university food service would come in and set up in the kitchen, and in the dining room the table was extended to the necessary length or taken out completely so that small, round tables could be placed in the dining room and connecting living room. For more formal dinners, a menu was printed and placed at each place setting. There was often a delicious sorbet between courses. Although Pop always watched his weight, stepping on a scale each morning and never fluctuating far from his ideal, he loved well-paced, extended dinners with time for conversation that went on and on.

At the large Christmas buffet parties, the entire first floor of the Carlton Street house was jammed full, and a refreshing blast of cold air ushered in each arrival at the front door. Pop would often skip eating altogether until the evening was over. Buffets were tricky for him because with only one hand it is difficult to both hold your plate and eat, but also he was preoccupied with greeting and spending time with the many guests. I remember the conversation being very relaxed and high spirited at the Christmas parties, with people from many different departments, and from the greater Boston community, with their spouses, merging in a merry hubbub. Bill Shannon, a professor at Boston University and regular *Boston Globe* columnist, had been the ambassador to Ireland. He and his wife, Elizabeth, the author of several books including one on their experience in Ireland when Bill was ambassador and another on the violence in Northern Ireland, *I Am of*

Ireland: Women of the North Speak Out, were friendly, near neighbors. "I wish you would have a word with your father about these glasses," Bill said to me on one of these evenings in a serious tone, holding up his drink. I looked at it dubiously, and he went on, "They should really not be so small."

At any party, I was always most delighted to see one of my favorite people on earth, Howard Gotlieb, the director of Special Collections at Boston University. Always tremendous fun, he was part impresario and part imp. Howard could be very grand when giving speeches or introducing famous visitors but also had a puckish sense of humor. His PhD was in history, but when strangers happened to ask what kind of doctor he was, he liked to tell them with great dignity, "I deal with the brain." One of his favorite gambits, often perpetrated at Locke-Ober or the Ritz, was to pull out a gift box wrapped in festive paper and ribbons while having a round of drinks before a meal. When he lifted the lid, a few neat rows of canapés (which he called blotters) were revealed, and he would proceed to pass these around to his guests, causing a few raised eyebrows from waiters, maître d's, and diners at neighboring tables. But no one ever tried to stop Howard.

When JRS came to Boston University, Howard Gotlieb was there, already building his great archive of twentieth-century memorabilia that has become a magnificent resource for researchers and biographers, as well as for students. He and Pop had both been at Yale and knew some of the same people, but their paths had never crossed there. John was tremendously impressed with Howard's achievement at Boston University, due mostly to his perseverance in pursuing artists, authors, and other creative people of all kinds, often before they were well-known or acclaimed elsewhere. He succeeded in building the archive with the force of his personality, as he worked with a very modest budget, unlike some curators of special collections at other institutions.

Under Howard's watch, the archive gained the manuscripts and memorabilia of playwrights, artists, musicians, historians, journalists, ballerinas, stage actors, movie stars, and on and on. These individuals of achievement were sought out by Howard and convinced by him that Boston University was the perfect home for their letters, journals, photographs, and other artifacts, a place where they would be preserved and appreciated.

One of Howard's collectees was Libby Holman, a torch singer and actress who left her magnificent house, Treetops, to the university. When we first arrived in Boston, there were plans to use the property near Stamford, Connecticut, for seminars and educational retreats. Our family got to stay there during this period, while Pop was getting an idea of what the place was like. This was before it was decided that the plans to use it for university retreats wouldn't work because of its distance from Boston and the cost of its upkeep. It was a gorgeous house that had a casual room for entertaining, with autographed photos of movie stars on the walls, opening out onto a terrace with a beautiful swimming pool. There were elegant gardens, and down a path nearby was a clay tennis court. The formal dining room had an unusual feature: it had no electrical outlets or light fixtures. It was designed that way intentionally to necessitate the use of candles.

Some of the most valuable and cherished papers in the Special Collection, now called the Howard Gotlieb Archival Research Center, are those of Martin Luther King, who earned his doctorate at Boston University. Coretta Scott King, hoping to consolidate her husband's entire collection in one place, sued the university. I was in court to hear the final arguments made by her attorney and by Earle Cooley, the chairman of the board of trustees at Boston University, representing the university, Howard Gotlieb, and the archive given to him by Dr. King.

Everyone was tremendously deferential to Mrs. King. She didn't have to sit on the incredibly uncomfortable benches where the rest of us sat. Anyone who has ever watched a trial at the old Boston Courthouse knows how excruciatingly hard the wooden seats are, like a Puritan instrument of torture. The bailiffs carried in a large, plush armchair for Mrs. King. However, it became clear that Martin Luther King had intended Howard Gotlieb to house and protect his life's work and the jury ruled in his favor. From the evidence, it actually seemed that Dr. King intended all of his papers to reside at Boston University, but no one was going to make a motion in that direction.

Howard made a great contribution to the social life at the university. His group, the Friends of the Library, not only turned out for the speeches and receptions in honor of the special guests who contributed their papers to the collection but also for social get-togethers that took place around these events. Some of these gatherings were held at the university or the Algonquin Club, others were low-key parties at Howard's apartment. Howard tended to make friends wherever he went. He naturally got to know his apartment neighbors, such as the great philosopher, John Findlay, who liked to regularly drop in on him and have a drink together. Howard was greatly amused when Findlay told him that he enjoyed conversations with Howard because he didn't have to think.

As the collection grew, it became clear to Howard that he required an aide, a factotum who could help with his great undertaking. It was Vita Paladino who answered his want ad, which contained the intriguing line: *Must be willing to work with celebrities.* Howard's splendid entertainments reached their height with Vita's help in the New Year's Eve celebrations of the millennium. For these there was dancing and the dinner tables were decorated with cherry blossoms. My dear friend Howard is no more. Over the years, Vita, who has recently retired, carried on, working with contributors and establishing creative programs for students so that they can participate in a hands-on experience of the collections. The young people enjoy pulling on white gloves and going through the files, examining letters, photographs, and other memorabilia.

One time, news anchor Jack Williams and his wife, Marci, arrived at a Carlton Street party from another event in a stretch limo. He didn't act super cool about it. Instead he asked if some of us wanted to go out and see it. So my husband and I and several others went out to see what it was like to sit in a stretch limo.

Jack was given short shrift by some during his first years in Boston, no doubt because of his blond good looks. Over time, he proved himself on the air and through his charity, Wednesday's Child, while still keeping his modest, mildly self-deprecating manner. He also became a friend of Boston University due to his association with Howard Gotlieb and the Friends of the Library. After an event, as Jack and JRS happened to fall into step with one another while walking across campus, some music wafted toward them, and Jack blurted out,

"Shostakovich," identifying the composer of the melody. Pop looked at him for a moment, sizing him up, and said, "Yes." They were friends from then on.

When there were major musical presentations in the living room at the Carlton Street house, the regular furniture was taken out and small golden chairs were set in rows facing the baby grand piano. The performers might be the stars of School of Fine Arts Dean Phyllis Curtin's opera program singing arias or Schubert's Lieder, the great pianist Anthony di Bonaventura at the keyboard, or some other extraordinary artist of the Boston University community or visiting from elsewhere. More casually, sometimes guests at parties sat down at the piano. Someone often volunteered to supply the accompaniment for carolers at Christmas, a good friend and Boston University vice president, Dean Doner, liked to play Cole Porter melodies at parties, and trustee Richard Joaquim and his wife Nancy could sometimes be prevailed upon to sing duets.

This was the same piano where the daughters practiced, and where Martha and Caroline had lessons. Poor little Caroline never enjoyed the piano much and I can remember seeing her sitting there, the very image of youthful suffering, as her very kind teacher rubbed her feet. The teacher held to the theory that it would relieve a headache to rub the toes.

One Christmas, my sister Judith's husband, Harry, sat at the piano and treated the family to an impromptu lesson on different types of syncopation. But the most astonishing and entertaining musical performance I ever witnessed there occurred when Chairman of the Board of Trustees Earle Cooley and his wife, Jean, broke into a rendition of "King of the Road," snapping their fingers while singing and dancing around the room.

16

Devotion to the Arts

Pop MADE ONE BIG CUT TO THE BUDGET WHEN HE DISCONTINUED football, a sport that was never really to his taste. This was long before Boston University became one of the leading research institutions studying traumatic brain injuries, and that issue was not one of the deciding criteria. The main reason was financial. The Boston University Terriers were not good enough at football to make money at it, and building the team up would siphon too much money away from his primary goal of improving the academic stature of the university.

On the other hand, he learned to enjoy hockey, as the Terriers had an excellent hockey team. He often took his children and grandchildren to games, especially when Boston University competed for the Beanpot. He learned to understand the rules of the game and supported the team, but he never loved the sport. When I attended with him, he would always call my attention to the great Zamboni as it smoothed out the ice, and he seemed to enjoy watching it as much as the action of each period.

His lack of interest in football and hockey may have been partly due to never having played them. He was more interested in baseball, a sport he had played. It was surprising that he was able to strike the ball with a bat quite well with only one arm, and he was a great fielder too, able to catch with a mitt, whip it off, and throw the ball in one fluid motion. Physical fitness (swimming, using a treadmill or stationary bike, and walking wherever he could) was something he valued for himself. He always enjoyed going to Red Sox games and liked following the ups and downs of each baseball season.

Besides improving academic standards, Pop's great vision was to transform the Boston University campus by rebuilding and revitalizing many of the existing buildings, building many more, and transforming much of the surrounding area. He mentioned his architectural endeavors at Boston University in the introduction of his book, *Architecture of the Absurd*:

> Although my knowledge of the history of architecture and my experience in studying buildings and drafting were useful when I taught classes in aesthetics, it never occurred to me that all I had learned from my father would be put to constant use as a university president. Oversight of Boston University's building program, including new construction, renovation and remodeling of existing buildings and the selection of architects and contractors, was an important part of my responsibilities. Our building program over a quarter of a century totaled 13,729,143 square feet. It included classroom buildings, science and research buildings, a school of management topped by an administrative center, several dormitories, a bookstore, convenience centers, a boathouse, a field house, a fitness center, and a 6,500-seat arena. It also included the construction of major medical facilities and the renovation and preservation of thirty-three elegant townhouses for dormitories and academic centers. In overseeing these projects my prior experience proved invaluable.

The only bookstore at Boston University had been the hard slab cement space in the basement of the George Sherman Union. It had been there forever, and it only sold textbooks.

John Silber had an idea for the Boston University Bookstore—to create something that was more than just a bookstore—to create a magnetic destination point in Kenmore Square. The impressive old building with its prominent position in Kenmore, holding up the famous Citgo sign, was perfect for the purpose, and the project would be so successful that the revitalization of Kenmore Square blossomed from its creation.

In the early 1980s, the Boston University Bookstore was planned as a multidimensional attraction for students and others in the community. Of course it had textbooks, but it was also a first-rate bookstore with classics as well as up-to-the-minute bestsellers that would attract authors giving book talks, and there were all sorts of shops included. You could browse housewares and lighting, or clothing, or foreign magazines in many languages, and there was a Viennese café on the top floor.

My dad wanted the several floors of the interior to elevate the mind and spirit of each visitor, and he felt it would be a point of pride for Boston University students. The architectural design of the interior included columns and beautifully detailed entranceways with richly polished wood for each venue on several floors. It was a great place to meet with friends and spend some downtime shopping or enjoying the coffee and delicious treats at the coffee shop. I know my kids and I loved to spend time there.

It was a great success in every way, and very profitable. Sadly this great attraction, this point of pride and identity for Boston University students, is no more. In 2018, the bookstore moved to a rather small, dark, fortress-like building on the western side of the campus. Perhaps shopping habits have changed, or perhaps the property in Kenmore Square became too valuable so that maintaining the grand old store was no longer feasible. At any rate, Pop did his best to create an inspiring environment for the students, the faculty, and everyone else who visited or worked in the Boston University community. Executive Vice President Joe Mercurio oversaw the bookstore project and the many other building and restoration projects during his thirty-eight-year tenure at Boston University.

Aside from architecture, Pop's heart was in the arts and all things cultural. He invested university resources in the arts as part of its trajectory toward an excellent experience for students, but this realm was also his passion. He was an artist. His first instinct when describing something was to draw it. He could draw people, animals, buildings, ships, anything from memory or from observation. What he saw transformed itself magically into the clean line on paper, and as a sculptor he molded true-to-life images from clay. He had a splendid singing voice, and for a time while he attended Yale Divinity School, he was a choir director. As a young man he also studied the trumpet, during one year of college giving his all to the instrument before deciding his talent was not good enough. Yet his interest in music never diminished.

In 1982, JRS established the Huntington Theatre at Boston University. With a beautifully refurbished theater near Symphony Hall, it was a real, professional theater company that gave acting students at the university a chance to participate with expert actors and directors. Pop loved the theater and was very proud of how beautifully it was appointed with velvet-cushioned seats and gold-accented designs around the stage. He loved to attend the performances, both those with professional actors in the lead roles and others that were entirely student plays. He took us as a family to innumerable productions there.

Phyllis Curtin, a beautiful and talented opera soprano recruited by JRS as dean of the School of Fine Arts, founded the Opera Institute at Boston University and also became a dear friend. With Pop, we often attended professional-quality student operas when they were staged at the Huntington Theatre or at the Tsai Performance Center, an excellent stage at the center of the Boston University campus. And once, my husband and I traveled to New York with my parents to see one of Phyllis Curtin's opera students, Haijing Fu, debut at the Metropolitan Opera. Phyllis Curtin was a marvelous teacher, and it was inspirational to attend one of her master classes at Boston University or at Tanglewood. She obviously cared for her students and continued teaching even after her retirement as dean.

Paul Montrone, with whom Pop shared a love of opera, was the president of the Metropolitan Opera. On the night of Haijing Fu's debut, he hosted a post-performance dinner party at 21 at which we toasted the success of the young star. My parents also enjoyed the Montrones' extravagant bocce tournaments each summer in New Hampshire. These house parties were beautifully organized with fun activities and prizes for several categories in the bocce games. In the evenings, the attendees would pilot a small fleet of classic wooden motorboats across the lake to the Wolfeboro Inn for dinner.

Once I had to call my parents during one of these weekends due to what seemed at the time to be a crucial family emergency. Paul Montrone, a larger-than-life character, answered the phone in his great booming voice. When I asked to speak with my dad, he could tell all was not well. Before he went to find Pop he said to me, "Whatever it is, don't worry. We have armies!" I could see why he loved opera. Paul Montrone's personality seemed to have stepped right out of one.

JRS greatly admired Derek Walcott, who joined the faculty of Boston University in 1981 and began the Boston Playwrights' Theatre, where graduate students can produce the plays they write. His epic poem, *Omeros*, was published ten years later, and shortly thereafter, Walcott was awarded the Nobel Prize in Literature. He continued to take a keen interest in his students, as well as writing poetry and books of his own. Pop gave all of his children copies of *Omeros*.

At Christmas, Pop often gave my siblings and me books by professors he esteemed and had recruited to the university. I remember receiving books and articles by Christopher Ricks, William Arrowsmith, Elie Wiesel, Rosanna Warren, and many others.

Although my dad and Christopher Ricks, an eminent literary critic and scholar, became friends, they nevertheless had ongoing friendly disagreements. Even now, years later, Christopher can't help complaining to me, "Why was John always inviting those ghastly conservatives like Roger Kimball to dinner?" It annoyed Christopher that his friend seemed to like so many conservatives, but it seems reasonable to me that politics did not determine Pop's friendships. He naturally wanted a mix of left- and right-wing voices, not only as friends, but to enliven a dinner table discussion.

Pop continually questioned Christopher's admiration for Bob Dylan. Our dad attended Christopher's lectures on Dylan, but his ear could not learn to appreciate the singer's voice or phrasing. Intellectually, he followed Christopher's elucidation of the songs, but Pop's heart wasn't able to make that leap.

When recruiting outstanding professors, including Nobel laureates, they were never mere ornaments meant to boost the prestige of Boston University. JRS was always looking for esteemed, prospective faculty members who would not only continue their research or writing, but would also delight in their interactions with students and be prepared to enthusiastically teach students and nurture their intellectual growth. Sheldon Glashow, with a Nobel Prize in physics, joined the faculty and became our neighbor just across the street from the back garden gate at Carlton Street. Martha often babysat the Glashow children. Whenever

I met Shelly at university events over the years, he was always most interested in talking about what his students were up to. I didn't understand half of it, but his love of teaching was clearly evident.

Saul Bellow, who came to Boston University with a Pulitzer and a Nobel, could often be seen with a shambling gait, making his way along Commonwealth Avenue, a benign smile on his face while deep in conversation with eager students.

In 1976, JRS persuaded Elie Wiesel to join the faculty. Elie would from then on divide his time between New York and Boston University, where he taught classes in the fall semester until his retirement in 2013. Among the eminent professors recruited to the university by John Silber, none was more sought after as a teacher than Elie. Ten years later, he was honored with a Nobel Peace Prize. Annually, Elie also gave a series of lectures at Boston University that were open to the public. My dad attended these lectures and introduced Elie at the first one each fall. Pop enjoyed the challenge of thinking of something new to say about him year after year.

Despite knowing of his reputation, when I once attended with my dad, I did not anticipate the reception Elie received at Morse Auditorium on the college campus. People came forward from the audience, waiting to speak with him and be near to him. There was a reverence for Elie that was highly emotional.

This reverence had to do with his experience as a Holocaust survivor, which he wrote about extensively, as well as his support for the survivors of many other hardships. Yet the classes he taught at the university were not on the Holocaust, as you might have imagined, but were focused on literature and memory. He had tried to teach a class on the Holocaust once but found it too emotionally difficult.

In 1982, Elie and JRS were both scheduled to speak at a conference on genocide in Israel. At the last minute, the Turkish government didn't approve of the Armenian delegation presenting a paper on the Turkish genocide against Armenians. Elie stood in solidarity with the Armenians, deciding not to attend, and the conference was canceled. Then, Elie and Pop agreed they would travel to Israel anyway.

Judith and Martha decided to tag along on this trip. On their way to Israel, Pop and my sisters stopped for a few days in Greece, where

Judith and Martha were afraid they might lose Pop when he insisted on climbing halfway down a rocky slope to get a perfect shot of the Parthenon. This was before the era of selfies, but even then, an avid photographer would risk his life to capture a perfect image.

When they arrived in Israel, a war with Lebanon was going on. Judith and Martha recall that every citizen was on the same team, with a feeling of purpose, mobilized to protect their world. For my dad and sisters who were visiting the country for the first time, it was a tremendous boon to have Elie, Marion, and their son, Elisha, as guides, and this proved to be a most extraordinary time to see the country. They also had a driver, who drove them all over the country, bouncing along the roads in a jeep-like car.

Driving to the Golan Heights, they stopped along a roadway where there were live minefields. The signs were clearly posted: *Stay out—Live Mines!* Pop got out of the car and went marching off to see what he could observe, as Judith and Martha shouted at him, "Daddy, please don't! Come back!" The car driver insistently calmed them. Speaking with serious urgency, he said, "No. He has to do this. He has to see this himself."

Pop told me that a most poignant moment for him was when they visited Yad Vashem, the Holocaust memorial, where Elie was able to show my dad the name of his Aunt Susie, inscribed in the list of Auschwitz victims. She and Pop's father were Ashkenazi Jews who had converted to Christianity. Pop only knew that his aunt was deported to Theresienstadt. At Yad Vashem, he discovered that Aunt Susie had been sent from there to the death camp.

My cousin Susanne, who is named after Aunt Susie, has recently learned from documentation that Susie had been sent away from Theresienstadt, a less severe concentration camp where many Christians and artists as well as Jews were held, because the Red Cross was planning an inspection. The Nazis did not want the inspectors to find it overcrowded. Susie was kept alive for many weeks at Auschwitz in case the Red Cross followed up to see where so many had been moved. But the Red Cross let them down and never came to look for them.

Once, Pop and I took the train to New York and stopped by Elie's apartment before taking him out to lunch. After he let us in, hardly even greeting us, we trailed behind him back to his desk. His hair was ruffled, and I imagined him before our arrival holding his head with both his hands, deep in thought. Before he spoke, he sat at his desk and scrawled a few lines. There was a keen tension in the way he could not leave his work and turn his attention to us until he drafted those final thoughts.

My father sculpted a bas-relief of Elie Wiesel's profile. It is one of Pop's finest works as an artist, capturing the characteristic contemplative look that is so well known. Cast in bronze, it is a brilliant tribute to his friend Elie.

17

Still Grounded

Breakfast at Carlton Street followed a regular pattern. Mother no longer cooked a big pot of hot oatmeal as she did in Texas, but she would make a large pot of coffee and prepare Pop's granola and fruit, resulting in his continual, ongoing complaint that the strawberries were too large and too white in the center. Why couldn't we get the old-fashioned small ones that were red and flavorful all the way through? He always yearned for an earlier, more idyllic way of life.

We didn't all try to sit down and begin together, but as we came in to eat quickly and rush off to school or other activities, Pop was there taking time over his coffee or tea as he whipped through several newspapers, marking them up or tearing out articles and whole pages. If you looked at a paper before he did, you knew better than to mess it up, and if you read it after him, you could expect gaping holes.

We ate breakfast and casual suppers in the room we called the eating porch. The name was probably a holdover from the screened porch where we took meals in warmer seasons in Texas. The eating porch in the Carlton Street house was a lovely sunroom surrounded by tall and wide French casement windows looking out on a small enclosed garden. To continue the garden theme, the one solid wall of the room had trellises and a small, carved stone fountain with a face that could spout water from the mouth.

Family meals in the evening, with everyone sitting down together, were the goal if our parents weren't going out or having guests at home. Sometimes the wait was excruciating if Pop was delayed at the university, but we waited for him, even if he knew he would have to go back to work for several more hours after the meal. I never had the impression that he came home for dinner out of duty. It seemed like there was a magnetic pull, that he wanted to be there with all of us together.

Pop held to the theory that it was good to make life more difficult, or at least less luxurious, for your children than your means might allow. He would explain later that this was meant to help us learn to handle adversity and fend for ourselves. So even though we lived in a mansion in Brookline, we never thought of ourselves as really deserving it. We felt lucky to live there, and we knew that our dad didn't own the house on Carlton Street. It belonged to the university and its size and magnificence were for the purpose of entertaining.

Our dad gave us very minimal allowances, and we negotiated necessary clothing with Mother as needed. I remember when I first went to college, Pop drove me out to the Wellesley campus and handed me a check that was to cover my expenses for the entire year. He told me to budget carefully and make it last until May. No one bought me supplies for my room either. I took a set of sheets and a towel from the linen closet and that was that. As it turned out, the money he gave me barely covered my books, so I took jobs babysitting the children of professors to earn some spending money, but that didn't accrue much surplus for entertainment. At any rate, as Pop was giving me the check, he told me not to forget that I was there at college to work hard at my studies, and not for fun.

On weekends and holidays at Carlton Street, if there weren't any parties scheduled, there would not be any maids or staff on duty, and we liked doing very much our own thing then and on celebration days, especially at Christmas. Everyone helped with preparation and Pop devoted some time to choosing special wines. Often, as we all got older, we would have a wine tasting, comparing a few choices from his well-stocked cellar. It was always a treat to go down to the basement with him, unlock the door and step into the air-conditioned vault. White wines came first, with a large proportion of the space taken by German wines with beautiful, ornate labels. The reds were stored in the section beyond in a honeycomb of bins where they rested on their sides. There were some very nice wines down there, but there were also lots of bottles for everyday use. JRS enjoyed finding good, inexpensive wines to stock up on.

Over the years, the "kids" took on more of the planning and cooking at family get-togethers. I remember two Christmases when David roasted a suckling pig in the kitchen's extra-wide oven. He made fabulous stuffing for these with pistachio nuts and dried apricots. Some years, JRS and Martha's husband, Michael, roasted huge rib roasts, while Martha perfected the horseradish sauce and popovers. All of us contributed dishes that were our specialties. Mine was broccoli drizzled with butter, garlic, and lime juice, which everyone, even the little grandkids, seemed to like.

The table in the dining room was often extended to its greatest length for our large assembly, with Pop sitting at the head of the table, near the buffet covered with cork mats to hold the hot dishes of delicious food. One thing Pop insisted on: there were always hot dinner plates even for ordinary meals. He couldn't abide warm food being served onto a cold plate. In Texas, they were heated in the oven, and at the Carlton Street kitchen there was a warming drawer.

Mother sat at the far end of the table, usually with some of the youngest grandchildren. Kathryn especially reveled in these feasts where she was not in charge. After all the meals she had prepared and served, she always said that anything cooked by someone else tasted better. She continued to be the mastermind of the feast at Thanksgiving until Martha and Mike took on the roasting of the turkey and major planning. However, she never stopped making her marvelous pies. No one ever made a lighter, tastier pie crust. Her signature pie was tart cherry, but she also made splendid ones of pumpkin, blueberry, blackberry, and boysenberry. When the pies were in the oven, she let the little kids or grandkids use leftover scraps of pie dough to make imaginatively shaped pastries sprinkled with cinnamon and sugar.

Our family truly got back to the simple life in New Hampshire. The house on Squam Lake was quite small, ensuring physical closeness, and not having a dishwasher, washing machine, television reception, or air-conditioning, it kept us down to earth. In New Hampshire, Pop was able to resume his outdoor yardwork with children, sons-in-law, and grandchildren as helpers, indulging in his love of physical labor. The grandchildren spent a few summers painting the one-story wooden house. It was an ongoing project, because once the last bit was completed, the first section was in need of a fresh coat of paint. He roused them in the morning with a reveille on his trumpet or with loud circus music on the stereo so they could eat breakfast quickly and begin work. In the afternoon, they were free to play and swim. Not everyone enjoyed these chores. One summer week, JRS kept my husband, Jim, so busy with chopping wood and doing repairs on the house that Jim swore he would never spend a vacation there again. Pop couldn't resist trying to get the most out of his strength and expertise while he had him captive there.

But it wasn't usually all work. There was normally time for hiking, swimming, sailing, and canoeing. Pop even bought a Boston Whaler boat so that the grandkids could learn to waterski. Pop's usual exercise at Squam was to swim across part of the lake. He didn't trust himself to do this safely, so he had one of the kids follow him in the rowboat, or if no one volunteered to row, he tied a life vest to himself and towed it along as he swam.

On these jaunts across the lake he wore the most disreputable swim trunks imaginable. They were quite old and had been designed in an era when men wore very short shorts. At one point they were falling apart and Pop asked me to repair them. I should have refused as a service to mankind, so he would have had to throw the hideous trunks away at long last, but that was one of my roles, mending Pop's clothes. He never liked to throw anything away, and on days when he didn't go to the office, he wore his old clothes.

My husband was often truly shocked that JRS would wear such ancient clothes even on special occasions, like Christmas. Shirts might have fraying cuffs and collars, and sweaters had the occasional moth hole that I had sewn up with yarn. He was never sloppy. The old garments were perfectly well laundered and pressed. They were just very old. This was very much a part of Pop's well-ordered life, adhering to time-honored virtues, a conspicuous one being thrift.

He loved it when I could repair some article of clothing. I think it was also a romantic Victorian image he had of a faithful daughter handily using her needle and thread to extend the use of a garment, like something from an old fairy story. For my part, I enjoyed the challenge. Once I delighted Pop by repairing a hole in a pair of his seersucker trousers. I took a small bit of fabric from a hem and sewed it in, from the inside, with the stripes lined up perfectly so the patch wasn't easily spotted. Another time, JRS had bought a pair of very fine kid gloves, and he asked me to customize the right one to fit his stub. I must have been inspired that day because I somehow reconfigured the glove to accommodate the exact shape. He loved that glove and I was very proud to see how he enjoyed wearing it.

I wondered what people thought when they visited the house in New Hampshire. On occasion, JRS would invite Arthur Metcalf and Marcia Hall or some other honored guests to stay for a few days. I particularly wondered about Arthur, who I knew was accustomed to living in a very grand style. My kids nicknamed him "The Monopoly Man" because the cartoon picture of the robber baron type on the Monopoly board game, with his bald head and silver mustache, looked like a caricature of Arthur, and also because he lived in a magnificent mansion with a great hall, drank gin from sterling silver tumblers, piloted airplanes, sailed yachts, and rode to hounds in a traditional hunting pink jacket.

Arthur was also known for his quips. Once when the massive fireplace in Arthur's great hall was smoking, Pop worried that it would damage the museum-quality tapestry hanging on the wall above it and suggested it could be hung somewhere else. Arthur replied that he wouldn't hear of it. As he put it, "A man's gotta live!" Frequently, when Arthur did things extravagantly, sparing no expense, he would remark, "Feed the cat another goldfish!"

Pop and Mother never worried about the house at Squam Lake being too modest, and from pictures of their little house parties there, it looked like they were having a very good time. Mother told me that Arthur enjoyed contributing to the meals by making elaborate salads, and Pop can be seen serving one of his favorite lunches. He liked to carve slices of smoked salmon himself, rather than buying it already sliced, and prepare a lovely large plate of elegantly arranged thin slices for each diner. The ritual of slicing the salmon, everyone looking on and conversing as he did so, added to the enjoyment of the meal. Social life always seemed to revolve around conversation over a delicious repast.

John and Kathryn would also sometimes entertain very modestly at the Carlton Street House. Sometimes they had another couple over for a simple meal, followed by watching something, perhaps a Jackie Mason video, on television.

In his early years at Boston University, JRS became acquainted with Don Perrin, the owner of several businesses and a supporter of many charities. Don owned a camera shop, Crimson Camera, in Kenmore Square that did business with the university. One time the shop's delivery truck was parked up on the curb near the beautiful old president's office on Bay State Road. Pop noticed the way the truck was parked as he walked by, and he stopped to yell at the driver, telling him to never park there again.

When Don heard about it, he went around to the president's office, and, having heard how his driver was treated, waited with some trepidation until he was called in. He was just hoping to clear the air so that his business could carry on. When the two men met, JRS was disarmingly humble and genial, brushing aside anything he might have said to the delivery truck driver and insisting that, of course, the truck needed to be parked somewhere for deliveries. Don Perrin was not the first or the last to discover that beyond John Silber's somewhat intimidating, aggressive manner there was a charming and approachable fellow. It was the beginning of a long friendship.

Later, Don Perrin, Brad Washburn (photographer, mountainclimber, and founder of the Boston Museum of Science), and other members of the board of the Photographic Resource Center were looking for a new home for their organization. They needed space to display exhibits, offer resources to photographers, and conduct educational programs. Don thought of Boston University and asked John if he would go out to lunch with Brad Washburn and him to talk about the project. Instead, Pop invited them to a lunch served at the president's office. The result was that the Photographic Resource Center found a place at Boston University, and resided there for forty years until the university needed the space and took it back in 2017, a few years after Pop died.

Colin Riley, director of media relations at Boston University, mused recently that he often recalls conversations he had with John Silber. He told me that once, when a news story asserted that my dad was intimidating, Pop explained to Colin that no one can intimidate another person unless that person agrees to be intimidated. In his view, it had more to do with the thin skin of the one who feels victimized than with anything done by the supposed perpetrator. I must say, I see a great deal of truth in that.

Another time, Colin was tracking down all of Pop's essays, in their original form, as they had been printed. The one essay on the list that was most elusive was a high school paper JRS had written. It was titled "Truth or Tact." Colin never found the paper, but he was fairly certain what side John Silber came down on.

Part of the regular routine was that the office staff sent Pop's updated schedule to Mother at the Carlton Street house, and this was updated further over the phone by secretaries or Pop. Sometimes when JRS called the house, he liked to put on a thick foreign accent to trick Kathryn. He particularly liked to pretend to be Henry Kissinger asking to speak to John Silber. He had practiced imitating Kissinger's voice ever since his time serving on the Kissinger Commission regarding Central America. Mother could usually tell, but that didn't stop him from trying. One time, Martha's new piano teacher telephoned and introduced himself to Kathryn in a thick, hard-to-understand accent, and she said to him, "Oh John, I know that's you."

18

The Office Culture

COMMENCEMENT WAS A NATURAL TIME OF CELEBRATION WITHIN the academic calendar. The garden party, or tent party as it often was, and the after-party when some lingered on, coming into the house to continue the fun and enjoy the delicious leftover party food, endured as the most festive event of the year.

A less formal celebration was the Fourth of July, a great feasting day when we invited friends. The large yard of the Carlton Street house was particularly well-suited to entertaining. With tall, solid fencing around it on all sides, it was a lush retreat from the surrounding city, maintained for many years by a gardener named José. Originally from Portugal, he had a thick accent and a luxuriant mustache even more flamboyant than that of Hercule Poirot.

One curious feature of the yard was a swing of an unusual design. It was originally created, not as a swing, but as a hangman's scaffold for the retirement party of Pop's longtime executive assistant, Julia Pratt. Such jokes and pranks were emblematic of the president's office culture. There was always some kind of riff going, and many of the gifts JRS received from his staff were elaborate gags. There was nothing he liked better. He loved to create these jokes and he loved to be on the receiving end as well.

Some of the products of this gaiety were hilarious. For many years, the Boston University public relations spokesman, Kevin Carleton, and Boston University photographer, Kal Zabarsky, produced a calendar with a funny depiction of Pop on it, and one year they composed a photo of John Silber as Napoleon, who incidentally shared a birthday with Pop.

The idea of creating these calendars began in 1989 just before the Chelsea partnership, in which Boston University would take on the management of the Chelsea Public Schools. As Kevin remembers it, Peter Schweich, who would later become the first principal of Boston

University Academy, went with JRS to a meeting about plans for the Chelsea project in order to record it, positioning himself up among the reporters. Peter noticed JRS was scowling and asked Boston University lawyer, Mike Rosen, to "go tell John he looks like shit and he's got to smile."

When the lawyer whispered the message, JRS turned toward Peter and stretched his mouth into a huge, exaggerated grin—which was immediately captured by a *Boston Globe* photographer. Of course the picture appeared in the paper, and made Pop look like the Grinch. But it gave Kevin an idea.

He wanted to get the picture fast, so he called Charlie Radin at the *Globe*. Radin, who was a Boston University graduate, COM class of '71, had been the first editor of the *Daily Free Press* and was a staunch opponent of John Silber.

Kevin said to Radin, "I need that picture." And as an incentive to make it happen quickly, he added, "It will embarrass Silber."

Kevin and Kal then attached that picture onto the 1989 Boston University Calendar, had it printed, and Kevin wrapped it in pretty paper with a big bow before giving it to Silber. "What the heck is this?" he asked brusquely.

"It's a present," Kevin responded, rather stating the obvious.

When JRS unwrapped it, he paused and looked at it very intently. Then he asked, "How much did you spend on this?"

"A couple of bucks."

Then JRS asked, "How much could you sell it for at the bookstore?"

Kevin replied, "I imagine we could sell it for at least $4.00 at the bookstore." To this, the driver piped up with, "More, if you sell it with darts."

Joe Mercurio, always protective, asked JRS if he was sure he wanted to do this. But Pop didn't have any doubts and the project moved forward. The shrink-wrapped calendar with the crazy smile was sold at the Boston University Bookstore next to the Ansel Adams calendars. And the ones of Silber with his smile sold out at $6.95 in just a few hours.

Peter Schweich took his copy of the calendar to JRS and asked him to autograph it. Pop asked him for five dollars. Peter looked befuddled, but he got a five dollar bill out of his wallet. JRS said, "Hell, if that two-handed Texan can get ten bucks, I ought to get five." This was at a time when Roger Clemons was charging ten dollars per autograph. JRS sent all the proceeds from that calendar sale to the Chelsea project.

Each subsequent year, Kevin Carleton found an amusing picture of John Silber for calendars that were sent to friends and family. And every year, Kevin sent a calendar to Charlie Radin of the *Boston Globe* as a courtesy.

When Radin requested an opportunity to interview JRS about the Chelsea project, he was told he could come in at four o'clock that day. In his typical fashion in those days, Radin's response was feisty and belligerent, "You're really messing me up!" It turned out he needed to pick up his daughter from kindergarten at that time. Pop's office shuffled some other things around and said Radin could come in at six p.m.

As you would expect, the interview began with sparring. But as they went on talking, Radin learned a few things about his subject. He learned what Silber was trying to do with Chelsea—and what he had long been working toward with his work on the creation of the Head Start program. Radin discovered that Silber might not be such an ogre after all.

As JRS said in an interview with Caleb Daniloff for a *BU Today* retrospective article in September of 2009, "Charlie Radin was a firebrand, but an intelligent, serious young man. I disagreed with him, but that did not mean I held him in contempt."

Then Pop explained how he saw the transformation of their association. "Over the years Charlie matured and became an increasingly responsible, thoughtful person whose journalistic efforts I can only applaud. The evolution of our relationship is not unusual. It is characteristic of the relation of father figures and teachers to their children and students. When adolescents grow up, as Mark Twain observed, they are astonished at how much the old man has learned in the intervening years."

In the early days of his career at Boston University, Kevin Carleton worked for then-Director of Public Relations Bob O'Rourke. One assignment O'Rourke gave him was to write an article about the Boston University Prison Education Program run by Professor Elizabeth

Barker. Because of her nurturing association with convicts, she was known on campus as Ma Barker.

Ma Barker didn't want to be interviewed. She was afraid John Silber would see the article, remember her involvement in faculty strikes, and put an end to the Prison Education Program. She tried to put Kevin off, saying, "You'd have to drive up to Norfolk." The prison was located there. Kevin assured her that that wasn't a problem. "I have a car," he said.

Ma Barker tried a different tack, warning Kevin that the inmates could be quite scary and dangerous men. Kevin deflected, "Those are my people—I'm from Brockton."

The article was set to appear in the weekly tabloid-style newspaper that was published by the university at that time, called the *World at B.U.* JRS came by the office and looked at the articles that were ready for print. He went through each one, acting like a fussy professor of journalism, finding fault with each one. Then he came to the story about the prison program. Kevin thought, "Oh, great! He's saving my skewering for last!"

But JRS surprised him, saying, "Now, this is good. A well-written story about an important subject." Pop then wrote a letter to Professor Barker saying, "I'm glad you are still doing the Lord's work." He knew she was not religious but he meant it in a positive way, and she knew that he did. JRS was always aware of the bottom line, and he was impressed by how much Professor Barker was able to do with a very limited budget.

President Silber was always invited to the prison graduation ceremony, but never attended as it took place at the same time as the Boston University overseas program graduation at Heidelberg. One year he was able to go to a special ceremony scheduled in the middle of the summer. Two of the top students, William "Lefty" Gilday, AKA "Machine Gun" Gilday, and Bob Heard, a Black Panther and a huge, imposing man, presented Silber with a wooden plaque, carved with a chain broken in two at the top. It was inscribed with the words, "We came in chains, but our education set us free."

Lefty said to their guest, "We finished our education here. To set us free we need a master's program."

JRS turned to Jon Westling and said simply, "Make it so."

Bob Heard, the former Black Panther, succeeded in earning his master's degree, and when he was released from MCI Norfolk, he became a counselor at the Pine Street Inn.

Each year there were also T-shirts printed with *Daily Free Press* cartoons mocking the administration and Silber. Pop would always bring some of these home after the senior breakfast where they were distributed. Sometimes the T-shirts commemorated major events in a light-hearted way. The year both George H. W. Bush and François Mitterrand spoke at the commencement, a cartoon of them together adorned the shirts. The grandkids loved these as well as the ones from the Department of Buildings and Grounds picnic, which had the beautiful old Boston University seal emblazoned on a different, brightly colored background each year. A few times, we got to attend this picnic with Pop for fun activities and the most delicious food, the best peppers and Italian sausages ever.

Pop manned the grill on July Fourth, often barbecuing a cabrito, a whole young goat, when he could get it. He also made two kinds of sangria for these parties, one red and one white. These were very high-octane drinks because they were not only made of red or white wine mixed with fruit and fruit juice; they also contained healthy doses of triple sec and other liquors.

In Texas, Pop would crown the evening by firing off some illegal Roman candles and bottle rockets in the street as everyone watched from the sloping, front lawn. In those days, Vartan and Clare Gregorian were sometimes guests. Back then, Vartan, who would later head the Carnegie Corporation, was a professor at U.T. He would say to everyone, "Just call me Greg," but everyone loved calling him Vartan because it sounded so exotic.

In Boston, there was never a need to indulge in contraband explosives. Instead, many of us walked to the river to view the city's splendid fireworks show. You could actually see it pretty well from the upper windows of the house or even if you stood on one of the picnic tables in the yard.

The guest list varied, but always included staff from the office. This was Pop's time to serve them and show his appreciation. Among these were Sam and Natalie McCracken and their children. Natalie was a writer for, and became editor-in-chief of, *Bostonia*, the Boston

University alumni magazine. Although she was seriously handicapped and needed to use crutches to get around, she seemed to be lifted above any physical obstacle by her smiling and intent interest in life.

Sam, a longtime assistant to my dad, was a great thinker, a great brain, who often wrote brilliantly for *Commentary* and other publications but who spoke in a way that was very difficult to understand. In appearance, he reminded me very much of the actor, Monty Woolley, a large man, with his mouth hidden behind an overgrown, scruffy mustache and beard. He sputtered and stuttered to such a great extent that it took some serious practice to learn to decipher his meaning. It was always well worth the effort though, as he was witty as well as brilliant. He often masked his extreme shyness by carrying a camera and spending a great deal of time behind the lens, focusing on people without having to look at them directly.

The McCrackens' daughter, Elizabeth, and her siblings often attended these Fourth of July get-togethers. She has since written several novels and short stories. My sister, Alexandra recently commented to me that back then Elizabeth "was probably studying all the human behavior going on at those parties."

It was our opportunity to become better acquainted with these people Pop knew so well and worked with every day. There were many assistants over the years. Pop sometimes invited them to dinner when they were going to be working late, but it was also nice to see them at a party. For many years in Boston, Julia Pratt was JRS's executive assistant. She had been at Boston University before he arrived, but not working with the president. Pop soon determined that she had the intelligence, skill, and manner that he would need to help him in the difficult job ahead. She also had the reserve of a true Yankee. Pop enjoyed teasing her, trying to break the façade and make her laugh. She clearly enjoyed this, too.

In more recent times, the executive assistants were Jennifer Horgan and Kelly O'Connor, who were very different from one another. Jennifer had a lovely gentle manner, and she was especially thoughtful in a personal way, visiting my mother on the many occasions when she was hospitalized and kindly helping me to revise my résumé when I was applying for teaching jobs. Kelly, with fiery red hair, was a tremendous fan of the Boston Red Sox. She attended every home game and even traveled to watch the team practice in Florida. For JRS it was like having an in-house ticker tape for the team. He could always get an up-to-the-minute report on how the Red Sox were doing.

Brian Jorgensen, who began as an assistant to JRS, was instrumental in creating the Core Curriculum at Boston University, a wonderful two-year humanities program of classes in art history, classics, classic literature—and with courses as well in the natural and social sciences. The Core was Pop's idea, but it was not something that could be dictated from above. A first draft of the curriculum, produced under College of Liberal Arts Dean Rufus Fears, was an unwieldy amalgam of courses suggested by interested faculty.

This excessively large assortment was then pared down and later refined by Brian and other professors committed to teaching in the program, including my husband, Jim Devlin. Under CLA Dean Dennis Berkey, the Core gained tremendous support, and with Brian's guidance as founding director, it became an acclaimed course of study at the university. Brian, a poet and author of short stories and novels, and his family were friends with my husband and me and our children. His son, Edmund, is a writer, as well.

Jon Westling and his family were often guests. Jon had a beautiful, mellow, cultured voice, and everything he said was thoughtful, well-formulated, and often memorable. And yet there was nothing snooty or egotistical about him. He was genial and relaxed, and genuinely enjoyed meeting and conversing with people.

It was well-known that he enjoyed riding a motorcycle, something that seemed at counterpoint with his esoteric interests. Those who knew him well were also aware that he enjoyed laidback evenings with musical friends who played guitars and other instruments while he maintained the rhythm performing on the washboard.

Jon began at Boston University as an assistant to President Silber and moved on quickly to become provost, and then executive vice president, in which position he took on the role of president when JRS was away. Jon Westling was president for an extended time when Pop ran for governor of Massachusetts. Jon Westling was then inaugurated as president in 1996, at which time John Silber became chancellor.

When these changes took place, the Silbers remained at the Carlton Street house, and a new president's house was made possible by a generous gift from the Marshall Sloane Family. The stately Gothic Revival property, Sloane House, just a block away on Carlton Street, was beautifully refurbished, furnished and appointed. Jon would serve as president until 2002 when he returned to teaching.

Joe Mercurio, who came to Boston University shortly after JRS arrived, chose to work there, among other reasons, because of the generous tuition program for employees that would allow him to take classes for free. He got his degree that way and worked his way up to the position of executive vice president, overseeing much of the growth at the university. He brought his family to our Independence Day picnics. I don't think there was anyone Pop trusted more, and he made Joe the executor of his estate.

Another frequent guest at the Fourth of July parties was Rev. Tony Campbell, who often brought his children, too. JRS had heard about this dynamic Black preacher with a graduate degree from Boston University's School of Theology, and went to hear him at his church in Roxbury. Our dad had not been a regular churchgoer for a long time, but he found Campbell's message inspiring and the energy of his manner engaging. Pop, along with several of my siblings, often returned to participate with Campbell's boisterous and actively involved congregation.

Conversations between Tony and JRS were lively and seemed intimately vital. I remember one time he was telling Pop that in the face of the terrible Black-on-Black, inner-city violence, he was teaching his children to never hurt, and especially never kill, someone of their own race. I found this offensive, feeling that he implied that it was okay to harm a white person, but I kept this to myself, not wishing to offend a guest. This didn't stop JRS. He pointedly asked Tony about it and they had a candid discussion in which Tony explained his view on the hierarchy of obligation.

Doug Sears and his wife, Mary, also attended often. Over the years, Doug worked in many different capacities at the university. Among them, he was an assistant to John Silber and dean of the College of Education. He is currently the vice president and chief of staff to the president at the university. During five of the twenty years when

Boston University managed the Chelsea schools, Doug became the superintendent, overseeing the project.

Doug says he got a big dose of every side of John Silber's personality. "What I most wish people knew about him is that he was the most fun and the funniest person I ever worked for. The amount of time wasted in the office on sheer fun was incredible. Also, he was a good sport when we played jokes on him."

19

The Campaign for Governor

It was no secret that JRS had political aspirations. There had been talk now and then since early years in Texas that he might one day run for office and that the ultimate goal was to become the President of the United States. There was a photo of our family sitting on the grass, taken artistically from above, for an article about JRS shortly before the move to Boston University that looked very staged. I thought, "So this is how it's done when families become political."

Even so, the discussions about the run and the decision-making were not a familywide matter. Our parents kept it very much to themselves until we were all invited to Faneuil Hall for the announcement. But from then on, it was as if the floodgates had been opened. Pop was in the news every day, and we were always in suspense to hear what he said next: the famous Silber Shockers.

I don't remember us using the term "politically incorrect" in 1990, though that is certainly what the Silber Shockers were. These statements were outrageous only because they were blunt and truthful, something a normal politician would never utter. JRS was such an extraordinary combination of super-intelligent, deeply learned, and astonishingly forthright. You don't ever get the full flavor of that combination from a sound bite or a snippet of a larger discussion. Pop always believed that truth mattered, especially spoken truth. How could the truth of an assertion be discussed and tested if it was kept as an unsayable, taboo secret? He called Massachusetts a welfare magnet, attracting people from far-flung places with tropical climates who would never have otherwise left them for the uninviting, frigid winters of New England.

People called him a racist for saying this, yet nothing could have been further from the truth. He had supported racial integration all his adult life, served on the commission that created Head Start, and opposed capital punishment primarily because it was disproportionately inflicted on poor non-whites. He simply did not see how Massachusetts could consider it fiscally desirable to actively attract people to the state with offers of welfare. He wanted to focus on getting people off the public dole through education and training programs, starting with nutrition programs for the very young.

JRS also said that, for mothers of young children, a job wasn't a better choice than staying at home if it entailed placing the kids in third-rate daycare. I remember *Boston Herald* columnist, Margery Eagan, railing against his lack of empathy for working mothers, but that was not the case. He had been talking about each mother making the best choice possible for her children and staying at home in the early years if at all feasible. His first thought was always to wonder what was happening to the kids and their development. He didn't hold with the view that women in the workplace deserved more praise than homemakers raising children. He saw child rearing as an honorable profession. That doesn't mean he failed to understand that for many women there was no choice. Many had to support their families, but he believed they should do their best to find excellent child care or their children would surely miss out in their crucial developmental years.

JRS impugned late-term abortion, equating it to giving birth and then killing the baby. He always loved babies. Babies and children, all that potential and such fun. He also put the needs of all younger people before the needs of the very old. As he put it, "When you've had a long life and you're ripe, then it's time to go." I think he really meant overripe. He didn't believe that extraordinary measures made sense for the aged. The press remonstrated against the Silber Shockers, but they also lapped them up. JRS got tons of column inches and evening news minutes.

Just getting on the ballot would be a great score, but as the Democratic Convention drew closer, the competition with former Attorney General Frank Bellotti was fierce. My husband and I and our family lived on a farm near Worcester at the time, and driving to political events that mostly took place closer to Boston was a trek, but we went to fundraising events at least once a week.

Mother and Pop even made a three-day fundraising swing through Texas, stopping in Dallas, San Antonio, and Austin. Attending the event in Austin were many old colleagues and friends including Alex Mourelatos, Louis Mackey, and Bob Solomon from the philosophy department at UT, Sam Dunnam, a local real-estate developer with a lifelong interest in philosophy, as well as Congressman Ralph Yarborough, Lieutenant Governor Ben Barnes, and legendary coach Darrell Royal. I imagine Frank Erwin would have attended as well had he not passed away almost a decade before.

The event in Austin was hosted by Lowell Lebermann, a Texas businessman. Blind from an early age, he was easily recognized due to his rakish eyepatch and companionable seeing-eye dog. Lebermann was involved in state and city of Austin politics, supported the arts and many educational endeavors, and did national fundraising for the Democratic Party.

The kids always brought along their homework as we eagerly made the long drive for fundraisers and debates. For one of the first debates, we were given only a certain number of tickets. So James, the youngest, was nominated to stay behind. He changed out of his suit, and settled down to watch television at the Carlton Street house while the rest of us went to the television studio.

When we arrived, Pop asked where James was and we explained that there weren't enough tickets. He said that was nonsense and sent a young driver for the campaign back to pick him up. Somehow, when the driver and James walked into the studio, my son was wearing a blue blazer paired with bright orange surfer jams. For a moment, I was horrified, but the very stylish young woman in charge of seating everyone said to him, "Happening threads, Dude," making his day.

Pop always did very well in the debates so far as winning arguments and proving points went, but he wasn't entirely tuned in to the whole other side of self-presentation. He was not impressed by Bill Weld calling himself a "slacker" and having his casual get-togethers with Howie Carr and other members of the press for the purpose of drinking mellow amber liquids, but many voters were. JRS didn't realize he could, and should, just relax a little, not work so furiously toward his goal, and thereby get further. This would be a modified version of the tortoise and hare lesson.

Television ads for the campaign were made by Bob Squier, who would go on to create political commercials for Bill Clinton and Al Gore. Pop sent us videotapes of the ads before they were aired, and we made comments about them as his in-house focus group. JRS had a seasoned campaign manager in Robert "Skinner" Donahue who had worked on the campaigns of Jimmy Carter and Ted Kennedy. Even so, with the many less skilled "pros" and the innumerable novice volunteers that joined our cause, the unwieldy operation was essentially amateurish.

I was worried when a commercial about Frank Bellotti seemed too insulting. I called my dad advising him not to run it because of the rough accusations. He thought the statements were true but agreed that the implications were too negative. His team was convinced that going negative was necessary. Pop called Bob Squier to cancel the Bellotti ad, but it was too late; the television spot had already aired.

Some of Pop's better ideas for commercials, such as ones in which he would speak Spanish, were filmed but never materialized. However, the negative ad may have been one of the elements needed to get the Democratic nomination.

When JRS first got into the race, he had to carefully consider who his opponents might be. One contender he felt some concern about was Boston mayor, Ray Flynn. Flynn, who could easily take a swath of the vote, kept saying he was thinking about getting in the race but then pulling back and not taking the plunge.

Just before the Democratic Convention in Springfield, Flynn announced that he might go out there—just show up and see if he had the support and could sweep up the nomination.

When the press asked about Flynn's statement, JRS didn't say that it was awfully arrogant of Flynn to presume he could jump in at the last minute and take the nomination. But he also didn't dish the humdrum pablum of wishing Flynn well. Silber's response was, "So Flynn's dance of the seven veils continues."

Pop also gained the support of several powerful contingents. He was backed by Senate President Billy Bulger and by Tom Menino, then the president of the Boston City Council, who would become Boston's next mayor. As Mayor Menino put it in his remarks at the event launching my dad's book, *Seeking the North Star*:

Our relationship flourished when in 1990 I got a call from John and he told me he was running for Governor. "Great idea," I said, "but it's late and I have a long relationship with the Attorney General." And even though my slate was neutral, everyone assumed, including me, we would go with Bellotti. John kept calling and come convention time, I ended up voting my delegation for John, giving him the margin he needed to get on the ballot. After that John ran the most exciting race for governor in my lifetime, and though he didn't win, his candidacy paved the way for welfare reform and increased funding for education. Oh yeah, my friend the former Attorney General stopped talking to me for about the next twenty-five years.

For our family, the convention in Springfield involved mostly hanging out in hotel rooms, a constant hubbub with friends and supporters dropping by, and anxious members of the campaign team keeping tallies, calculating and re-calculating possible results.

The next week, after winning the nomination, JRS invited Frank Bellotti to the Carlton Street house for breakfast. Bellotti accepted the invitation, but when he arrived, proud and dignified, he said he was getting over a stomach bug and couldn't eat anything. He would not even accept a cup of tea. I rather admired this symbolic act of refusing to break bread with JRS after he had run that negative ad, but for Pop, as the party's nominee, this didn't bode well for how helpful Bellotti and his people would be in the election.

There has been a great deal written about how temperament was Pop's Achilles' heel. Steve Kornacki, a journalist from Massachusetts who earned his degree in political science from Boston University has become well-known for his enthusiastic gesticulating when he works with interactive election maps on national television. Not long ago, Kornacki reminisced about John Silber and the temperament issue that was covered during the 1990 campaign by Natalie Jacobson. While Jacobson's interview appeared to have been done just days before the election, when Pop was up in the polls and predicted to win,

Kornacki, like many other people, did not know that the interview was taped more than a month before the election.

It was curious how it came about. A month before the election, when Pop was down in the polls, Natalie, along with her daughter, took Natalie's dog to be seen by my sister, Alexandra, who is a vet. Remarkably, Jacobson had never seen Alexandra before that appointment, nor from what I have been told, at any time since. During the appointment, Jacobson offered Pop what was termed a casual getting-to-know-the-family interview for an upcoming Sunday show. We accepted what we thought was going to be a lighthearted interview. Perhaps we were naïve political rookies because the interview did not go as we hoped and expected.

On the long drive into town, my husband, Jim, asked if we had any topics that we were prepared to talk about. I hadn't even thought about being prepared. My parents had said Natalie wanted to film a casual family meal, nothing more. Jim persisted, asking if it wouldn't be good to at least have some ground rules, or some idea of where we might like the conversation to go.

I planned to pull my parents aside and ask them about this when we arrived, but that turned out to be impossible. The television crew had already wired both JRS and my mother for sound before we got there, and even worse, my dad looked haggard. He had just gotten over a flu and his skin color didn't look healthy. On top of that, Skinner Donahue wasn't there to help guide the proceedings. Another less experienced and less forceful manager, Michal Regunberg, was present.

What followed was more than an hour, maybe two, of interrogation, moving from room to room, that involved continual pressing questioning by Natalie. I don't recall any light conversation about sports or hobbies. I remember when she was asking for our view on women taking on traditionally masculine jobs, I explained that I believed standards should not be altered to make that happen. I said that if a female firefighter needed to climb a ladder to rescue me, I hoped that she would be a big, strong woman. But I didn't notice any warmth or understanding in Natalie's eyes as I spoke, and I wondered why the conversation was going in this direction at what was supposed to be a casual dinner.

We felt as a family that she crossed a line when she asked James how he felt when the people at school said terrible things about his grandfather. It must have been pretty overwhelming for a second-grader to have a beautiful lady offering sympathy if only he would unburden himself to her, but he just said, "I mostly hear good things." I think that the rest of us at the table were adversely affected as we felt she was pushing at us nonstop with her questions. We were all becoming thoroughly annoyed with Natalie, and the disgust Pop felt was clearly evident on his face and in his whole demeanor. Rather than play for the cameras as a seasoned politician should do, he made a few choice comments that bristled with contempt.

It is a well-known method of news media to conduct a long inter-view and only use a carefully edited portion that makes the point they are after. But what happened in the election of 1990 seemed extraor-dinarily calculating. One negative morsel aired soon after the interview took place, and it took a while for the ruckus from that to die down. Then, a month later, when Pop was leading in the polls shortly before the election, the carefully pruned segment saved for just that purpose hit the airwaves: a bombshell just before the vote. And, of course, the effect was magnified because Weld and his PR guy, Dick Morris, played the worst part of it repeatedly on TV up to the election.

Perhaps we should have suspected the damage was done when Natalie was packing up to leave with her hours of tape in the can. My impression was that she seemed gleeful, almost giddy, as she looped her arm through mine while she was saying her goodbyes, and almost danced us across the living room toward the front hall.

And then she started gushing about "the Welds" and how she would soon be interviewing them. I found the way she said "the Welds" in a hushed, reverent tone to be very telling. I thought it spoke of her awe at their wealth and social position, and I think we should have known then to expect the worst. JRS has said since that if he had it to do again, he would not have let Natalie into the house for more than fifteen minutes. You learn so much during a campaign, but the learning curve can be steep and costly.

Natalie's interview with the Weld family had the casual feel that she had told us to expect for ours. Though it was filmed later, it appeared ahead of ours. In it, Natalie appeared to drop in at the Weld house just as Bill Weld was in the middle of cooking up a family breakfast for his kids. Obviously, she could not have shown up then because she and her team would have had to arrive before that to wire Weld for sound. We felt as a family that Natalie clearly did her best to present him in a golden light.

There was another moment when I thought the press seemed to be rooting for the Weld team. After one of the debates, Mike Barnicle told my husband and me about the first line of his column that would appear in the next day's *Globe*. To paraphrase, Mike knew that it was National Magic Week because John Silber had made the opposition disappear.

We didn't take the *Globe* out on the farm, so I called a friend in Concord the next day to ask her to save the column for me. However, when she looked in her paper, there was no Mike Barnicle op-ed essay. I was disappointed and thought I must have misheard when he expected it to run, but later, I found the piece in the *Globe* at my parents' house. What was going on? Was my friend mistaken or was it possible that the *Globe* had not run that column in the suburbs because the powers that be wanted to limit the influence of a column that was too strongly in favor of John Silber? Do newspapers have alternative editions for different regions? I don't know enough about it, but I would be curious to know how that works.

Perhaps Mike Barnicle could investigate someday and find out what happened to his column.

William Weld, looking rather the worse for wear, popped up in the 2016 presidential election as the Libertarian VP candidate. I think his ticket would have done better in the race if he had been the candidate for president and the wacky Gary Johnson had taken the less prominent place. Weld ran again in 2020. This time, running for president as an anti-Trump Republican, he entered some of the primaries with the hope of gaining a few delegates from President Trump, the Republican incumbent.

One very good thing that Bill Weld did as governor of Massachusetts was to appoint John Silber to head the board of education. I was driving in East Boston not long ago and noticed the Early Childhood Education center named after Pop there, a lasting reminder of the good work he did. JRS loved visiting any classroom and speaking with students of all ages, but he especially enjoyed the youngest ones.

In another foray into public education, Pop instituted an unprecedented experiment in which Boston University took on the management of the Chelsea Public Schools for twenty years. Who else would have taken on the challenge of bringing excellence to a school system in crisis? Who else would care enough or be brave enough to put his reputation on the line and give it a try?

Pop had already created a program at Boston University for motivated graduates from the Boston Public Schools. Quoting Mayor Menino again:

> In 1980, when most people were saying that the City of Boston was dying because of the Boston Public School system, John Silber created the largest scholarship program in the country for public school students. The Boston Scholars program is an enduring, living legacy to this man and his vision and his commitment to a City he loved. Every year, 100 Boston Scholars attend Boston University and the students, the Boston Public Schools, the City of Boston, and Boston University all derive extraordinary benefits from this amazing program.

In 2013, the Boston Scholars program at Boston University was renamed the Menino Scholars after the mayor.

The testing of all students in Massachusetts along the way and at the end of high school, in order to graduate, was and continues to be controversial. JRS never saw it as testing the students; he saw it as testing the school system and holding it accountable. He felt teachers who weren't able to teach should not be protected by the teachers' unions. He hated the practice of passing students along from grade to grade and then out the door without ever delivering the education the schools had promised to provide. He saw each student as an individual who deserved a chance to succeed.

In stories about John Silber, there is often a question about his temperament. But frankly, I don't trust people who don't get angry. To me it means that they don't care that much about anything. Or else, it can mean they hide their anger and turn it into seething resentment that they use in an underhanded way against others.

Looking back on that 1990 campaign, Pop realized that his temper had probably lost him the election, which was so close. But I believe that if anyone were to watch the whole Natalie Jacobson/Silber interview tape, uncut and unedited, they would at least find John Silber's reactions more understandable, and therefore less damaging.

20

Temperament

WAS IT BECAUSE OF THE ARM? IT HAS BEEN OFTEN ASKED IF POP'S explosive temper and his vehement quest for excellence were an effect of being born with a deformed arm, an overcompensation. When I was about twenty, I met someone whose father had the exact same type of stub as Pop's, only it was on the left side. To my surprise, his personality could not have been more opposite. He was a bland, jocular fellow, with no interior volcano ready to burst, and no catapult toward excellence either. He was an uncomplicated man, happily settled in his mundane career. So was there any relationship between my father's stub and his temperament?

I often felt sorry for Pop because it seemed to me that he missed so much by not being more easygoing, with his energetic force, ready to charge in and challenge you and his flashpoint temper always ready to flare. So, he often didn't see people at their best. He didn't get to know timid people very well if they couldn't relax and be themselves in his company. He saw them either struggling to express themselves, or with their back up against him, resenting his challenge.

With bold people his rough manner didn't matter. His quicksilver temper didn't stop them or intimidate them into hiding themselves. But it was terrible when he verbally attacked someone who wasn't up to it. On a few rare occasions, I saw him harangue one of his subordinates, raising his voice and looking ferocious and angry. We kids also saw him do this to each other time and again. To see him yelling like that was demoralizing for everyone concerned. Afterwards, Pop would work things out, and feel all was forgiven, but, no, it wasn't. If you were ever on the receiving end of one of those diatribes you would not soon forget it, and you would hold it against him, however charming he might be afterwards.

I was always aware that it was necessary to be ready to do battle. The way I kept it in my mind was to always be metaphorically ready to hit him over the head with a lamp. Ready to get his attention and push back. It sometimes worked. Other times I just had to let him be until later when he was in a better humor.

As kids, we were more likely to be on our best behavior when he was around, and he missed out because of this. He didn't get to see all the whimsical ways that David would clown around because he was too nervous to relax and completely be himself with Pop. That's why Pop could hardly recognize the David with a cockney accent, holding up his Guy Fawkes dummy as he good-naturedly accosted strangers at the Tube station near our house in London, and why he was so surprised by David's impersonation of him at the student party. These were unusual happenings. David thought he was off on his own at the Tube station and somehow he was inspired the night of the party and let it rip before he got too shy to impersonate Pop in his proximity. David was able to express himself later, as an actor, in a controlled setting away from our dad's influence, where Pop could see him at a safe distance, from the audience.

Pop missed out on a lot of his kids' silliness. We were silly with him when he was in a silly mood, but he was rarely able to come upon a scene at home without distorting it like a great rushing wind. That doesn't mean he was always confrontational. He just brought all his standards, judgements, and high expectations with him, and that could dampen the high spirits of the room.

I believed that I acquired an insight into Pop's angry façade when I came down with rheumatoid arthritis at age thirty, suffering from it tremendously for several years. My hands were in so much pain that I was unable to do simple, ordinary things. I even resorted to pulling up the bed covers with my teeth. I had to get my kids' help with everything around the house from cleaning to cooking. At the same time, I didn't want to worry them and didn't tell them I was sick. I preferred for them to think that I was a stern task master, and even a bit mean. I supervised them as they vacuumed, loaded the washer, and assisted in making dinner. I'd say, "Okay, give the tomato sauce a stir and then fill the big pot with water and put it on the stove."

It occurred to me that Pop might be doing something similar. The last thing he wanted was for anyone to think he was disabled. He wanted to prove himself in the world and had no time for self-pity, even less for the pity of others. He would much prefer to be thought fierce. He didn't have time to waste and felt he must push constantly to accomplish his goals. I can imagine him thinking to himself, "Go ahead and think I'm a son of a bitch, but you're sure as hell not going to think of me as handicapped!"

There was a hierarchy of people he treated with deference. Those who were accomplished and powerful he felt a natural respect for. Anyone who did a job well, whether they were an artist or a manual laborer, he acknowledged and appreciated. It disappointed me that he often treated rude people with more respect than I felt they deserved. It was the old "hit him over the head with a lamp" scenario that I had noticed he responded to positively. On the other hand, he tended to look down on self-conscious and introverted types who might become tongue-tied in his presence and refused to get in the sparring ring with him.

Pop said to me admiringly more than once, "You're a fighter. You don't care if you get your teeth knocked out; you come right back for more." And one of his fondest terms of affection was to call one of us "Tiger." When cheering me on, he would say, "Go get 'em Tiger!"

I wish he could have been his amiable, relaxed self more of the time. When he was laidback and easy, no one was more fun. I remember when I was quite young, regularly holding on to his ears as I stood behind the driver's seat when Pop was at the wheel. I felt like I was involved in the driving decisions. I would tug to the right if we were going right and tug to the left if he turned left. It was like holding the reins of a horse, but even more cozy. I have recently found out that my sisters did the same thing with our dad. Pop loved those physical, emotional connections.

He also liked to take hold of us affectionately by the ear at odd moments, even when we became quite grown up. He would handle the ear as if he were modeling it in clay, rubbing it between his fingers and thumb, feeling along every rim and crevice. He said that he could blindly identify each of us by our ears.

He could also turn on us ruthlessly without any warning. Judith and I were once goofing around when Pop walked into our room, and looking around critically, he spied our Girl Scout manuals. The way he went through those pages, questioning every mark we had made and every claim of competence we had declared was like an inquisition. Yes, we had been very casual, seeing how many badges we could try to earn without really working too hard. I remember explaining to Pop that for the Collector's Badge I was collecting little rubber erasers shaped like animals and cartoon characters. You can imagine his fury.

One of the controversial issues on campus was visitation in the dorms. He didn't like the idea of boys and girls visiting each other in their rooms. Aside from obvious safety measures, he did not want to be a party to, or responsible for, sexual liaisons between students. He wanted students to work hard and focus on studying. For this reason, he also didn't want to allow cable TV in the dorms. That he might have been able to keep it out seems like a quaint notion now. The mores of the age were against him.

His was a more scholarly model for student life. He felt students should bury themselves in their books and not waste time. Aram Chobanian, who was president of Boston University from 2003 to 2005, took the opposite view, giving students access to all the technology that was available. Technology of all kinds is now so thoroughly integrated into our lives it would be impossible to think of separating college students from it.

At home, Pop would be furious if he caught any of us studying in front of the TV, but Mother never concerned herself with where we studied, and she certainly would not enforce his rule against it. Maybe that made Pop even more fierce. He knew he was one man, standing alone, holding back the dam of mediocrity with no ally.

Fortunately, our dad's vices were paired with corresponding virtues. Pop was a passionate man, not a cool one. He cared deeply for his family, his friends, and anyone he heard of whom he thought was deserving. If you were in trouble, you couldn't find a stauncher advocate. He would put himself on the line for you, offer carefully thought-out advice, and often help with money. There are many high-minded people who won't lend money, but when friends were in need, Pop either gave or lent money (sometimes a great deal) with no real expectation of return. The person he lent it to might be the same one who'd gotten a tongue lashing from him not long before.

We might hear about all this because Pop did not have a strong sense of privacy except about truly intimate relationships or attributes. One time during the governor's race, a reporter asked him if it was true that his son was gay. Pop responded belligerently, "Why do you want to ask me that? Why don't you ask me if *I'm* gay? And then I'd tell you it's none of your damned business!" But on many other subjects he was very open. In this, he was different from our mother who guarded all personal details closely. So far as Pop was concerned, anyone might know almost anything about him. In part this was due to his honesty, a simple forthrightness about most things. At the same time, it was essentially pragmatic. He was busy getting things done, and he had a lot of helpers, and was not concerned with keeping secrets of his own or those of others. He couldn't constantly worry about who was listening to what.

It could be aggravating when I had been keeping my rheumatoid arthritis a secret, and someone I didn't know well came up to me and asked, "How's the arthritis?" Also, we could always hear a great deal from Pop's side of a telephone conversation. We overheard his advice when he helped friends and relatives of friends with serious legal problems. One summer in New Hampshire, we heard all about a friend's business having trouble, and our dad lending a very large sum of money so it wouldn't go under.

That's why, whenever we had a secret, it was Mother we told. She could be counted on to keep it and not even tell Pop if we didn't want her to. When we needed to talk to Pop about something we needed him to know about or help us with, we often went to Mother first. My sisters and I can all remember sitting in the big leather chair in the corner by our mother's desk, in her study. There, we would tell her everything. To tell Mother, you didn't have to think it out first, or put it in the best way possible. You could just let it all out. Then, sometimes, you would be ready to tell Pop yourself, and sometimes she would do it for you.

Pop often remarked on how different he and Mother were in temperament. As he put it, "We make more sense together than we do individually." Even on occasions when Pop was at his worst, I always had a different perspective in reserve, derived from my early days hanging out and chatting with him in the morning while he shaved. Then he seemed invariably mellow, so I always knew his soft side was there. It was sometimes hard to reach, but it was definitely there.

Top: Kathryn, Ruth, Caroline, and Alexandra in the yard at the Carlton Street house. *Bottom:* David with JRS and Rev. Tony Campbell in the backyard at the Carlton Street house. Silber Family Photos.

Top: Fourth of July party in the yard at the Carlton Street house. *Bottom:* Martha's husband, Mike Hathaway, looks on as JRS mans the grill on the Fourth of July. In a few years, they would trade places and Mike would do most of the grilling. Silber Family Photos.

Top: David carrying a smoked turkey on the Fourth of July. *Bottom:* Pop took this photo of a family party in the yard at the Carlton Street house. *Front row, left to right:* Jim, Rachel, Caroline, Kathryn, Judith with Mary Beth, Mike with Martha; *second row:* Marc, Alexandra, Ruth, James; *top row:* David and John.
Silber Family Photos.

Top: Photo of David taken by Justine Devlin Eoff while visiting him in New York City. *Bottom:* Sculptor Sergio Castillo with JRS in El Escorial, Spain, summer 1984. There are three Castillo sculptures at Boston University, including his *Free At Last,* inspired by Martin Luther King, Jr.'s "I Have a Dream" speech. Silber Family Photos.

Top: David took this picture of Alexandra, Ampee, Charles, Judith, and Rachel at Monticello on our infamous cross-country trip with Ampee. *Bottom:* Caroline, Martha, and Ruth in the front hall at the Carlton Street house.
Silber Family Photos.

Top: Pop carving the turkey in the beautiful dining room at Carlton Street.
Bottom: For us, this was a small family group for Thanksgiving. Silber Family Photos.

Top: Headshot David attached to his resume in the early 1980s. *Middle:* Artistic shot of David. *Bottom:* Ronald Reagan shakes David's hand as cast of Broadway production of *Aren't We All* with Rex Harrison and Claudette Colbert performs at the White House. Official White House Photograph.

Top: Ruth clowning in the kitchen at Carlton Street while Caroline doesn't notice. *Bottom:* David, Charles, and Kathryn in the kitchen at the Carlton Street house. Silber Family Photos.

Top: Mary Beth and JRS next to the antique intercom in the kitchen at Carlton Street. *Bottom:* JRS playing what he called a "pocket trumpet." This is a photo he gave to Ampee. Silber Family Photos.

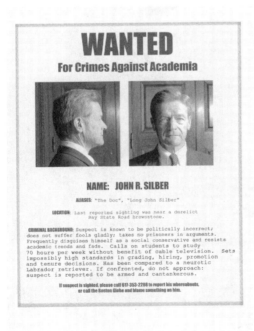

Top: JRS as Napoleon, with whom he shared an August 15 birthday. This image was attached to the Boston University calendar one year—created by BU Public Relations VP Kevin Carleton and Boston University Photographer Kal Zabarsky for friends and family. *Bottom:* Humorous calendar for 2006. Also created by Kevin Carleton and Kal Zabarsky.

Top: JRS walking to the office on Bay State Road meeting the philosopher, John Findlay, 1973. *Bottom:* JRS always thought Dean of Student Affairs Staton Curtis looked like Henry VIII, so he presented him with a portrait of Henry VIII with Staton's face Photoshopped in by Jerry Schuerger working with Photo Services and the Graphic Design Office. Boston University Photography.

Top: James, Kathryn, Mary Beth, JRS, and John. Here are my parents trying to sit for a formal photograph while the grandkids make comical faces. Boston University Photography. *Bottom:* Judith with Kathryn in Bremen, Germany, summer 1984. Aside from trips with the whole family, my siblings and I enjoyed the undivided attention of both parents when we took turns traveling with them. Silber Family Photos.

Top: Ruth and JRS in Grindelwald, Switzerland, on a ski trip. Silber Family Photos. *Bottom:* JRS looks on as Roger Clemens autographs his book for Mary Beth and John at the grand Boston University Bookstore in Kenmore Square. Boston University Photography.

Top: JRS with children at the Boston Public Schools and Boston University PE Co-op. Boston University Photography. *Bottom:* JRS visits the Chelsea Early Learning Center, 1990.
Photo by Kalman Zabarsky for Boston University Photography.

192

Top: John and Kathryn with Governor Mike Dukakis and his wife, Kitty, and Senator Ted Kennedy and his wife, Joan. *Bottom:* JRS with Billy Bulger, president of the Massachusetts Senate. Boston University Photography.

Top: JRS and the Kissinger Commission on Central America meeting with President Reagan. *Bottom:* Ronald Reagan with JRS and Kathryn Silber.
Official White House Photography.

Top: Prime Minister Margaret Thatcher with Kathryn Silber and Ronald Reagan. Official White House Photography. *Bottom:* George H. W. Bush and Françoise Mitterrand with John Silber. Both heads of state spoke at the 1989 Commencement. Boston University Photography.

Top: JRS on *Firing Line* with William F. Buckley. Boston University Photography.
Bottom: JRS with Boston Mayor Ray Flynn.

JRS announces his run for governor of Massachusetts at Faneuil Hall.
Back row: Caroline, Jim, Rachel, JRS, Alexandra, unknown, and David.
Front row: Mike, Martha with Joseph, Kathryn, Mary Beth, John, James, and
Jewell. Boston University Photography.

Top: Campaign rally on Marsh Plaza. Boston University Photography.
Bottom: Ted Kennedy joins JRS at the new Chelsea Early Learning Center, 1990. Kal Zabarsky for Boston University Photography.

Top: Photographers can ask you to do embarrassing things during a campaign. *Front row:* Mary Beth, Martha holding Joseph, and James. *Center row:* Kathryn and JRS. *Back row:* Alexandra, John Alan, Mike, Rachel, and Jim. Photo taken for *People Magazine* by Ken Regan/Camera 5/Regan Pictures, Inc.
Bottom: The end of the race. Fred Sway for Boston University Photography.

John took time off at his brother's ranch, Bullis Gap, at the Big Bend after the election loss in 1990. Photo by Paul Silber.

Top: Paul and John at Bullis Gap. *Bottom:* JRS target shooting at his brother, Paul's, ranch. Photos by Stevin Hoover.

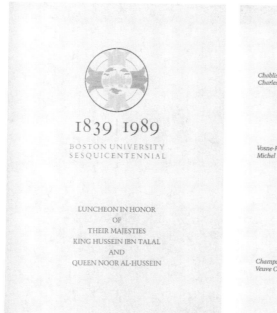

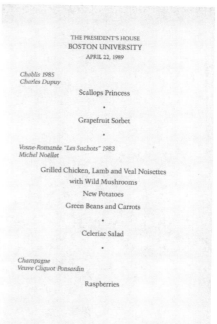

THE PRESIDENT'S HOUSE
BOSTON UNIVERSITY
APRIL 22, 1989

Chablis 1985
Charles Dupuy

Scallops Princess

·

Grapefruit Sorbet

·

Vosne-Romanée "Les Suchots" 1983
Michel Noëllat

Grilled Chicken, Lamb and Veal Noisettes
with Wild Mushrooms

New Potatoes

Green Beans and Carrots

·

Celeriac Salad

·

Champagne
Veuve Cliquot Ponsardin

Raspberries

Top: JRS with Alistair Cooke, Isaac Asimov, and Elizabeth Westling, 1989. Boston University Photography. *Bottom:* Menu for luncheon party for King Hussein and Queen Noor. Dinner parties had printed menus, and there was usually a lovely light sorbet course.

Top: JRS with choral conductor Robert Shaw during a rehearsal of *King David* at Boston University. *Bottom:* Party for King Hussein and Queen Noor of Jordan at the Carlton Street house. Left to right: Kathryn, King Hussein, Jim, Queen Noor, JRS, and Rachel. Kids in front: Mary Beth, James, and John.
Boston University Photography.

Top: JRS with Israeli PM Yitzhak Shamir, 1991. Boston University Photography.
Bottom: JRS with Jon Westling and Trustee Melvin B. Miller. President Silber at a
press conference announcing the trustees' decision to approve Jon Westling as next
BU president on January 12, 1995.
Photo by Kalman Zabarsky for Boston University Photography.

Top: JRS with Elie Wiesel, 1998. Pop introduced Elie at the first lecture of his series each year. *Bottom:* JRS honored with the Distinguished Eagle Award for 25 years of distinguished service in his profession since becoming an Eagle Scout, with (*left to right*) JRS, William Weld, and Billy Bulger, 1997.
Boston University Photography.

Top: JRS and Martha sailing at Squam Lake. Harold, Mammy's husband, helping guide the boat into the dock. *Bottom:* Ruth and John on a float. Harold and Mammy in chairs; *Standing:* Caroline and Alexandra holding Mary Beth. Silber Family Photos.

Top: Rachel holding Mary Beth, Martha, John, Caroline, and Ruth on the deck at Squam Lake, John showing us his loose tooth. *Bottom:* JRS and Bill Cloherty, "The Giant Leprechaun," washing down the boat after a sail at Squam.
Silber Family Photos.

Top: Kathryn and Marcia Hall preparing dinner in the Carlton Street kitchen.
Bottom: JRS at the helm of Arthur Metcalf's sailboat, the *Veritas*.
Silber Family Photos.

Top: JRS at the helm of *Veritas*, with Kathryn by his side. Silber Family Photos.
Bottom: Howard Gotlieb, Rachel, and Jim at Howard's annual summer party at The Colony in Maine. Photo from Howard.

Top: JRS with his mother, Jewell, and Angela Lansbury, 1981. *Bottom:* Howard Gotlieb, Gene Kelly, JRS, and Kathryn at the Gotlieb Center's American in Paris Ball, 1975. Boston University Photography.

210

PART THREE

Patina

Adversity and Character

21

Time with David

WE DIDN'T KNOW WHAT WAS GOING TO UNFOLD AND SPREAD INTO our lives during the next year when Marc, David's partner, called my parents with the idea of planning a surprise fortieth birthday party for him. Mother and Pop were happy to be asked to plan the large celebration at Carlton Street.

The house looked beautiful that night. Round tables with white tablecloths and flower arrangements were set up in the dining room. The chefs were busily preparing the delicious feast and the waitstaff was standing by. We greeted David's friends, many of whom we hadn't met before. But then David and Marc didn't arrive. For the first hour, it wasn't too bad. We chatted and got to know each other. Then, at some point David called to tell us the heavy traffic was delaying their progress, so he and Marc couldn't tell when they would get into Boston. As the time stretched on, David's friends relaxed into companionable conversation in a large circle of chairs and couches in the living room.

At one point my husband and I, standing with Pop in the living room doorway, were stunned as my dad surveyed the party guests and wondered aloud, "How many of these young men will die of AIDS in the next few years?" We were shocked by his blunt insight. It entirely changed the cozy scene in our view. It was like looking at doom to think of that terrible plague, hovering over these unprepared young men, intent on taking hold of some random number of them. But I didn't break down or burst into tears. That would come later. On the blissful night of the party, we still believed that my brother and his partner were keeping each other safe.

We didn't know that almost ten years earlier, when David and Marc were first learning about AIDS, they went together to be tested, and the results came back HIV positive for both. They then decided not to inform their families, in order to have as much of a normal life as possible. David told me later that besides not wanting to make us suffer through an extended period of time, he also thought we might somehow blame him. I felt stricken to think he would expect me or any of our family (did he mean Pop?) to be less than entirely sympathetic, and he assured me that he felt his apprehension had been unfounded.

When David and Marc finally entered the house two hours or more late, my brother was embarrassed and dismayed by the large assembled group, but Marc had obviously told him about the party somewhere along the route, probably before the phone call. I say it was obvious because they entered through the front door, something we never did when arriving by car.

I have always been averse to surprise parties for this very reason. Even under the best circumstances, it is impossible for the surprised honoree to be prepared enough to properly enjoy the event. But the party was meant well, and after David excused himself to freshen up for a few minutes, the evening turned out to be full of warmth, a loving celebration with toasts and good cheer pouring forth for David and Marc. Marc told me later it was like the wedding they never had.

But soon we would be spiraling down into the doom foreshadowed by Pop's observation on that night of the party because, shortly thereafter, David came down with esophageal cancer. He saw some doctors in New York, but Pop encouraged him to come to Boston and see some more. We still didn't understand the siege we were facing. Cancer, okay, we could deal with that. Get the best doctors on the case right away.

But it wasn't going to be okay. On the afternoon my brother came home for a series of doctor's appointments, there was a dinner scheduled for a visiting professor that evening, and Mother had set a place at the table for her son. David was furious with her and told her rather sharply that he wasn't there to be entertained; he had cancer. Mother was hurt. She didn't know the worst and hadn't wanted to exclude him. She and Pop could not skip out on their commitment and she had thought David might enjoy the conversation. She called me, and I came to Carlton Street to keep him company and eat dinner off trays in the play room. David wasn't able to eat much, though. The cancer was making his throat close up.

Over the next few days, it all came out. AIDS. Facing the incurable disease, with no hope, was a terrible death sentence. It felt like a physical blow. Mother was perhaps stricken the worst. She seemed ill, almost as if she had a bad case of the flu. I was able to keep going about my normal routine, but would break into tears every time the thought of it came relentlessly back into my head. Pop concentrated on getting the best doctors and finding out all he could about the available treatments and possible cures. Alexandra actually had found out David had AIDS before the rest of us learned of it because she had called and asked him point blank about it. She said it explained a lot for her. She believed it accounted for David's frequent trips home, his interest in all that we did, and his apparent lack of a driving ambition for his own career.

As David became ensconced in Boston, Marc frequently came for long weekends at first, and then stayed on as well. Pop introduced Marc to a friend with an architectural firm in Boston who gave Marc some work in his office.

My parents settled David in my old room, the one next to them, so they could hear if he needed anything in the night, and Marc was given Alexandra's old room that connected through a shared bathroom. As difficult as that time was, I nevertheless feel so grateful for it. Grateful that David came home. Grateful I was able to spend part of each day with him. Sometimes this involved taking him for treatments or to see doctors when Pop wasn't free to do so, or else just hanging out. It became the primary object of each day to find things David could eat, tempting little meals that were easy to swallow. He was losing weight and it was a constant struggle to combat this. This part of the new routine was the most like our old jaunts around town in younger days, but without the cigarettes, both of us having long since quit. We went out for soups and cheesecake and ice cream sundaes. But he never really gained any weight. We made valiant efforts, but he kept getting thinner.

The first thing David did when he realized he would not be returning to New York was to buy a large, bright orange hibiscus from Mahoney's Garden Center on Memorial Drive, one of his favorite places. His early adventures with Pop, going to dig up small trees for our yard, had kindled in him a lifelong ardor for making things grow. A room without living plants was impossible. Whenever he was home, he liked to walk about the yard with the magnificently mustachioed José and hear his plans for the flowerbeds. He was still able to do this when he first came home, and on into that last summer of his life, his favorite thing was to cross the driveway and then the lawn to see José's impressive dahlias blooming there. By the end of that summer, he no longer felt up to making what then seemed like a great expedition. I found him, one day, at the open side door, just leaning wearily against it and looking out at the yard. I asked if he wanted to go out, but he said he was just getting some fresh air. While he waited, I went out to the yard and brought him two dahlias, one spikey and purple, the other tender and rosy. David put these in an art deco crystal bud vase we found at the back of a shelf in the larder. It had been discarded because the rim was chipped, but a small chip never stopped David from appreciating something.

Before he started chemotherapy, he went to the University Barber Shop and told the barber that his hair would be falling out because of the treatment and he just wanted it all taken off, a buzz cut. The barber, John Zizza, who had cut Pop's hair for so many years, said he could do a little better than that, and he gave David a cut that was buzzed short over most of the head, but left a charming bit of flattop at the front. This was one of the innumerable kindnesses that we encountered from the many thoughtful people whose path crossed with David's during that difficult time. One of the most kind was Spencer Frankel, a family friend and David's dentist, whom he saw when he was in Boston. David had told him as soon as he found out he was infected, so as not to spread the illness, and Spencer then took it upon himself to keep David's secret for ten years and help him learn more about ongoing research and treatments he could get in New York.

Another friend who was immensely helpful was Aram Chobanian, then the dean of the Boston University Medical School. He had contracted esophageal cancer many years earlier and survived. Aram had kept his illness a dark secret at the university because he feared the community would marginalize him if they knew. Instead of going to Boston University doctors, he went to Beth Israel. He also resorted to wearing a wig until his hair came back. When David came home from New York, Aram was unstinting in his help. The fact that he had survived the same type of cancer was encouraging for David, and Aram made it a regular part of his routine to check in with my brother by phone or to stop by and see him.

Many friends sent cards, letters, and gifts. Howard Gotlieb gave David a giant stuffed baby chick from FAO Schwartz. It was just adorable and the softest, most huggable thing in the world. Vartan and Clare Gregorian sent spring bulbs that would bloom in David's room. Alexandra's mother-in-law sent cut, long-stemmed roses of an unusual variety that David had admired when visiting her garden in Texas. I was fascinated to watch as he took each stem, made a fresh cut, and dipped it in growth hormone before planting them all individually in small pots, to root them for his own garden, an eventuality he planned for even as it became obvious it would never come.

Some people were not so kind. There were a couple of encounters with pushy reporters who wanted to get the scoop on John Silber's son with AIDS. When David was pestered trying to check into the hospital, I heard him lie, saying he was not related to *that* Silber. Pop was less than honest with journalists as well when he told them he would find time to talk about it later.

Most of the visiting nurses who came to the Carlton Street house to take care of David were the best of the best. True saints of modern life, they treated their patient and all of us suffering around him with attentive tenderness and compassion. However, there was one officious nurse who gave me a lecture about not being so afraid of AIDS, saying that you can't catch it and it's fine to be more hands-on than she thought I was being. The trouble is that AIDS, while not communicable by touch, is nevertheless a disease magnet, so that someone with AIDS inevitably falls ill to several other ailments.

Besides the cancer, David also had meningitis and CMV, a virus that was causing him to go blind. CMV can also cause blindness in your unborn child if you catch it when pregnant, and Martha, Alexandra, Judith, and I were all expecting at the time. My doctor had scheduled me for a test to see if I was susceptible to the virus and would need some kind of preventive treatment, or if I already had antibodies to it. But in the meantime, I miscarried and put off attempting to have another child. Alexandra lost her twin pregnancy, as well. She said she had thought the twins would be a consolation to her, but as it was she lost both, and she felt David's loss was worse.

The OJ Simpson trial was a tremendous distraction from all the medical imperatives, and my brother was fascinated with the case and watched it all on television at home and in the hospital. He would say to the television, "Oh please, Marcia Clark, don't twirl your hair." Any diversion was welcome, as some of the treatments were brutal. Through it all, David suffered the pain and dread with tremendous courage and grace. He was resigned to his fate and after that first day of his arrival when he had chastised Mother for expecting him to join the dinner party, I never heard him complain or speak sharply with anyone. Once, when Pop and I were waiting outside David's hospital room while a medical team attended to him, we just looked at each other helplessly as his anguished cries came from the room. He was in terrible agony, but the worst we heard him calling out was to repeatedly moan, "Oh man. Oh man."

The one time he lost control was when he believed he could hope for a reprieve from the cancer that was closing up his throat. He underwent surgery to have a mesh tube, called a stent, installed. It was designed to keep the passage open. David was so excited about the prospect; he was euphoric the day after the surgery. When Howard Gotlieb and his friend Bill Adams stopped by the hospital to see him, David frightened them with his frenzied tears. He had put his emotions on hold for so long that he had something like an emotional breakdown that day, after the operation. He proudly showed his visitors the beautiful color picture of the stent with its intricate mesh design, the object that allowed him to hope. The tears streamed down his face as he feverishly expressed his yearning to live. Sadly, this stent turned out to be a chimera that soon revealed itself as a nightmare when the cancer started growing right through the mesh and closing in his throat again.

We got to know some of David's friends a little better as they came to stay when they were able. Stacy, a buddy of David and Marc's, was an early visitor, shortly after we first heard the bad news and while Mother was still sick with grief. Stacy took charge of making appetizing tea trays for both David and Mother. Another friend, Franklin, and his partner, Dave, stayed over sometimes as well, and all three visited with

David later when he was in the hospital for a while. Franklin brought a lovely bedside lamp to give David a break from the bright, hospital fluorescents. The lamp cast a soothing golden glow on the sterile room.

I, like David, was mostly able to keep my composure once I accepted our fate. I stood by sympathetically, but without joining in, when Judith had to leave after a visit, and cried in David's arms as he tried to console her. My turn came when David and Marc were discussing plans for cremation with their friend, Stacy. She agreed to take charge of David's ashes, and the plan was that she would also take Marc's when the time came and sprinkle them somewhere together. I listened in horror and then burst into tears. David held out his arms to me and motioned them to leave us for a moment, explaining to them, "She didn't know that I'm dying." I was barely able to choke out, "It's not that I didn't know. It's that I can't stand it."

Throughout those last months while David lived at home, Pop no longer seemed like a force to be reckoned with. While he could still talk to doctors and intellectually consider with David what his options were, he was in some ways halting and inefficient. He mostly seemed to wander around the house aimlessly during that time. He would lend a hand by washing dishes or emptying the dishwasher, something that always needed attention with extra people in the house, but unlike his usual self, he seemed almost inept.

When Mother regained her strength after the first shock, she became a strong gentle presence, the mother of our childhood. Her purpose was clear: to take care of David and make him as comfortable as possible. She had a twin bed placed in the hall by David's door, to be even closer in case he needed her. And when her firstborn died, she helped the nurse bathe and powder him, and dress him in a fresh gown. Then, when the nurse left, she stayed there alone in the dark, beside his bed, and sang lullabies.

The plan was for David to be cremated at the same time that a prayer breakfast was going on for him elsewhere. I was disturbed by the thought of his body being burned, so I skipped the prayer service, going instead to the crematorium at Forest Hills where I asked them to delay. Later, at home, when it was agreed that we would bury David rather than cremating him, it felt like such a relief to be able to keep him in some way. In my high school acting days, Pop had always thought I should play the part of Antigone. It felt like I was taking on that role in earnest for David.

The family and a few others assembled on an icy morning beside David's coffin at Forest Hills Cemetery. Pop's friend, the scholar Christopher Ricks, read a poem by Tennyson about a son who dies before his father. I had felt a bit guilty for interrupting David and Marc's original plan, but cremation had seemed terrifying to me at the time, and it was extremely kind of Marc to understand and go along with the change. Mother expressed her relief with her characteristic humor, saying that she was glad she would know where David was and he wouldn't be riding around in the backseat of Stacy's car.

I remember looking at Marc during the graveside prayers and noticing how cold he looked. For the past year, he had always seemed so robust compared with David who was withering away, but standing there by the open grave, Marc looked weak and lost and afraid. A few months later, he was gone, too. Taken by a ruthlessly swift infection. Marc's parents confided to Mother and Pop that they were grateful we had buried David so that they could bury their son, as well.

When we had the memorial service for David, I don't know how Pop mustered the strength to speak. Somehow he managed to stand and remember his son, honoring the memory of his imaginative boy.

22

Shipwreck

I REMEMBER MOTHER BECOMING ENERGIZED AND TAKING CHARGE when we decided against cremation for David. Pop had gone in to the university after the prayer breakfast, so she called him there to talk it over. Kathryn was dressed very casually, but she didn't even stop to change when she got off the phone. She just pulled on her fur coat and she, Judith, and I set out in the bitter cold for Forest Hills. We were unreasonably elated on that drive. It was perhaps a reaction to having had such bad news day in and day out for over a year.

As we got out of the car to go into the office at the cemetery gates, I felt like laughing because Mother looked so comical in her mink coat and navy blue Keds. All the same, I didn't laugh at her when we got down to business. I marveled at the way she expeditiously went about choosing the plot, driving around to see the choices, and determining that it would be a space for as many as twelve occupants. When I questioned needing so much space, her assured reply took my breath away. "For John and me, and anyone else in the family that wants to use it."

Perhaps it is morbid to be planning for your own death, but it consoled her to think that David would not always be alone there. Afterwards she said that perhaps it seemed like being a Pollyanna, but she felt so lucky even to have experienced so much pain because it resulted from loving so deeply and caring so much. Still contemplating her own inevitable passing one day, she said, "When I die, I don't want anyone to be sad." And with a mischievous humor she went on, "Play classical music because I don't like it very much." Then, more seriously, she added, "Don't play 'Home on the Range.'"

Everything had changed during David's illness. Our parents' social life had contracted dramatically during the ordeal and, in the aftermath, Martha and I helped fill it out. Mother and Pop usually came to my house for Sunday dinner and to Martha's on Saturday. We made these events festive, with music and delicious food. Martha and her husband, Mike, and their kids often prepared humorous menus for their feasts.

Martha's daughter, Ella, had been born in the month before David died. I was at the hospital with Martha for my goddaughter's birth, and minutes after it, we had called David to tell him about his new niece. He had been eager to hear the news as soon as possible. Around the same time, Judith gave birth to a son.

David took an interest in all his nieces and nephews. My oldest, John, will always remember the exciting several days he spent seeing the sights with David in New York City when he was about seven, and Justine, my husband's daughter, recalls fondly when she traveled there by train to explore the city with David while staying at his apartment. David's godson, Martha's son, John David, seemed especially drawn to David in his last days. Although he was only three years old, it was as if he intuited that this was his last chance to talk to his uncle. My brother said he particularly regretted not having children of his own, but he had a wealth of nieces and nephews, and he bequeathed his property near the Berkshires to them.

In the wake of his death, the grandchildren helped Kathryn and John carry on. There were two brand new babies in the family—Martha's daughter, Ella, and Judith's son, Isaac—to bring some interest into their lives. From then on, we did not slack off either. Ten more grandchildren were born between then and the millennium along with a first great-grandson, Andrew, the child of my son, James, born just after, in 2002. My youngest daughter, Claudia, born two years after David died, helped bring the colors back into my life as well. It seemed like happiness was possible again, that, perhaps, this low-key simple domestic pattern could go on and on.

I guess my dad and others realized that the time would not be so generous. In the spring of 2001, Boston University presented Kathryn with an honorary degree and held a tremendous tribute celebration for her. On that festive evening, Jack Williams introduced numerous speakers who expressed their appreciation for her kindness and generosity over the years. Both Martha and I made speeches that night, as well.

Then Mother's steep decline seemed to begin with a fall. But that can't really be true. That was just when my taking serious notice of it began. Unfortunately, before the accident, she was already taking Coumadin, a blood thinner, which exacerbated the damage of her injury. The doctor's appointments seemed routine before, rather than necessary to hold back catastrophe. When I arrived at Carlton Street one morning to help Mother color her hair, something I did for her regularly, she had a badly bruised eye. She was planning to cover it with an eyepatch and go out to dinner that evening. I went ahead with what I had come to do, coloring her hair and then blow-drying it, but it was clear something was wrong. She was pausing at odd times and sometimes used the wrong word in a sentence. Even so, I knew she would dread going to a hospital and didn't feel I could betray her directly, so I waited until I got home to my own house before calling my dad to tell him.

What followed was one operation after another. It was as if she was trying to go through the menu of the hospital and try one ailment from each category. They needed to shave part of her head for the first operation, and it made sense to cut the rest of her hair short. She also stopped coloring her hair then and it turned to a lovely pale silver. This was her new look. It suited her well because it showed off her nicely-shaped head and when she washed her hair it would fluff up like the down of a baby duckling.

While Mother was in and out of hospitals and rehab, Pop tried to insist on her quitting cigarettes, and, perhaps, to encourage her while also showing off his own self-control, he gave up the cigars he dearly loved to demonstrate his support. Smoking was the underlying cause of most of her maladies, but Mother was wily in her stubborn refusal to quit. If Pop was with her she would refrain, but whenever she was on her own being driven somewhere by university drivers, Tony LaGrutta or Richie Ford, she would ask to stop at a pharmacy or supermarket in order to buy the contraband.

When Pop was driven by anyone, even professional drivers, he was never a docile passenger. He was always second-guessing what the driver did and suggesting better strategies for getting through traffic. Tony and Richie each had their own way of repelling these assaults. Tony was a former New York City cop. His banter with Pop was cutting, like what would be served up at a comedy roast. At first I was a little intimidated by his gruff manner, but on better acquaintance he turned out to be a secret softie. His manly demeanor kept Pop in check, and a true regard developed between them.

Richie was more show than tell. If Pop was saying to go one way, Richie would sometimes do as asked, but if he thought he knew better he would smoothly go the other way and put Pop through turmoil until he saw it turned out well. Richie was a great reader and always had a book with him. He and Mother often made recommendations to one another. When Richie had just read Stephen Hawking's *A Brief History of Time*, he was talking to my parents about the Big Bang as the beginning of the Universe, to which Pop responded with a Socratic question, "What banged?" It's a simple query, but it gets right to the important point if you are looking for origins.

Eventually Kathryn gave in and quit smoking, but only because she became so ill, and all of us, including Tony and Richie, were on to her tricks.

My parents also settled into a quiet companionable existence then. They went out to very few events and Pop was often the one to put together something for them to eat in the evening, or else they went down to the pub on Beacon Street that had some delicious comfort food offerings, such as Irish stew. On Mother's last birthday, we had a big family party for which I baked two birthday cakes. The ones I made were a specialty of Mother's family that I had learned from Mammy. There were ripe banana slices between the golden vanilla cake layers, and the entire outside was iced in caramel. At first I thought it was ridiculous that I had prepared the extra unneeded cake as we only finished one that night, but I was glad when I heard that Mother and Pop relished having another slice every evening during the next week.

Claudia loved visiting with her Grandmama, and they always found a way to play together, even in the various hospitals. Sometimes Claudia pretended to be a doctor, Dr. Coleman, a name she borrowed from Jamie Lee Curtis's character in *Freaky Friday*. At six years old, in her excellent handwriting, she once wrote down a list of her medical observations, such as: *The patient prefers sweets and does not like to exercise.* Mother was delighted when one of the real doctors found this list and was puzzled by it for a moment.

In the meantime, Jon Westling had unexpectedly resigned, and Pop was filling in for his longtime associate and successor as president at Boston University while the search was on for a new leader. Pop favored one of the candidates, Daniel Goldin, a former NASA administrator. Many professors and trustees supported him as well because it was thought he could bring in grant money and lead the university in the direction of major physics research. Pop, aware of his own diminished vigor, had high hopes for Goldin. His take-charge style promised to get things moving and shake things up. Little did Pop know that Goldin's shake would be seismic.

The only time I ever saw the man in person was when he gave a speech in the ballroom, Metcalf Hall, on campus. He left the audience of Boston University supporters and faculty rather confused, not knowing how to react. This wasn't the well-spoken, learned sort of president we had come to expect. John Silber's speeches, always fascinating, were sometimes blunt, but they were eloquent and often intellectual as well. Jon Westling, without the usually requisite doctorate, had nevertheless always spoken with urbanity and well-expressed erudition.

This Daniel Goldin seemed lacking in culture. He also seemed unprepared and awkward, as if he were winging it and had hardly bothered to learn anything about Boston University. He kept going on and on about Bette Davis's Oscar. It must have caught his eye as he passed by its glass case on his way through the building. And yet, as he floundered for something to talk about, he clung to Bette Davis. He didn't seem to know anything about her either. He kept calling her "Bett" Davis, pronouncing it in the French manner, the way it might be sounded out, as if he didn't know her name was pronounced "Betty."

I think Pop was a bit distracted during that speech because it was the first time Mother had gone out to an event in a while, and she was noticeably infirm. He hovered beside her, making sure she was comfortably seated, and he enjoyed watching as she was greeted by so many friends who hadn't seen her lately.

Then all hell broke loose a week before Daniel Goldin was officially going to take on the job, when his list of planned, massive firings began to circulate. Why had JRS ever backed this dynamo that wanted to take a wrecking ball to his beloved university? He had mistaken Goldin's character. Admiring the man's forcefulness as a replacement for his own waning powers, Pop thought he was helping to usher in a new era of his own style. However, some of his own statements from early days at Boston University came back to bite him. His younger self had extolled the importance of "getting rid of the dead wood." Goldin might have said the same thing, but this fellow was no tree surgeon, ready to prune and shape and nurture. He was revving up his chainsaw and perhaps a bulldozer as well.

The trustees had to scramble to block him before he officially took over as president. In the end, they had to pay out a million and a half to make him go away. It cost Pop dearly as well. Although he retained his position as president emeritus, he was forced to move out of his office space in the grand new floors of the Rafik B. Hariri Building.

Most of the Hariri Building houses the Questrom School of Business, but the top three floors accommodate the meeting room for the board of trustees and the university's executive offices. These arrangements had evolved over time. Originally, the president's office had been at 147 Bay State Road, and the trustees' meeting room had been there too, but other executive offices were located in other brownstones up and down Bay State Road. When the trustees met over several days, twice a year, there was always a party at the president's house on Carlton Street as well.

Richard Joaquim, who had been with Boston University since the 1960s as coordinator of performance functions for the School of Fine Arts and manager of the Boston University Theatre, later became the director of university programs, and subsequently became a trustee. It was his idea that the trustees should meet away from the campus, and for this purpose he proposed his resort in Scottsdale, Arizona.

JRS considered the idea and said they should ask Arthur if meeting in a more relaxed atmosphere, away from the university, would be a good idea. Arthur Metcalf, who was chairman of the board of trustees at the time, suggested they put it to a vote. The result was that the trustees voted overwhelmingly to meet once a year at the Scottsdale Conference Resort.

The Scottsdale meeting turned out to be a wonderful time, and they also got more done than ever before. As usual, there were three days of meetings, but many arrived days early and stayed days after. They had a chance to get to know each other, without name tags. After the black-tie event on the evening of the third day, JRS said to Richard, "This was the most successful trustees' meeting we've ever had. We need to set it here for next year as well." And JRS put his arm around Richard's shoulder, in his very characteristic affectionate way, and said, "You should never have left Boston University." To this, Richard replied, "John, that's bullshit. You would have fired me." They both laughed, but this exchange had a kernel of truth. JRS wouldn't have fired him, but the respect he had for Richard in his separate, successful life was different from the relationship they would have had if Richard had remained a subordinate.

Richard would also be the one to suggest the ambitious transition and transformation of the president's office when it was moved to the Hariri Building. The School of Business, named for Allen Questrom, had left the three top floors (7, 8, and 9) empty. Richard met with JRS and said, "The way things are now, you have executive offices that are half-assed up and down Bay State Road. We need donors to feel they are giving to a worthy cause. It must be impressive. To raise vast amounts of money you need a suitable place. You can't be taking prospective donors in and out of small brownstones. You must think like the English thought in the eighteenth century. Think like Princeton, Harvard, and Yale."

Arthur Metcalf donated an impressive amount to opulently finish floors eight and nine. The cost of finishing those two floors was the most expensive of any office buildout in the city of Boston at that time. However, when the seventh floor was completed with more modest workrooms and offices for assistants and secretaries, the moderate cost for this floor was included in the project, bringing the price per square foot down to something more reasonable.

Umberto (Bert) Marcucci was chosen to design the ambitious top two executive floors of the building. When Marcucci thought of connecting the two floors with a staircase, JRS asked him to use Ed Masterman as a model to test the size of the structure and make sure it was on a grand enough scale because of Ed's stature as the tallest trustee, at around six-and-a-half feet.

Then, when studying the plan for the staircase, Martha's husband, Michael Hathaway, assistant VP of Campus Planning and Construction, had concerns that the ambitious plan had gone too far and insisted that they create a mockup of the staircase and see how it fit. When the scale model was built, it was clearly too large for the area, crowding out other requirements for space and movement. The plan was then readjusted, reducing the size just enough, while still effecting a grand staircase.

JRS went to New York to look at furniture. When he saw the price, he asked, "Do you really pay this amount?" Richard replied that it was necessary to pay so much for this quality.

The finished space with magnificent furniture and antique rugs was grand indeed, combining nineteenth-century warmth and splendor while secretly accommodating up-to-date technology. Everything was so opulently appointed and on such an imposing scale on these floors that Mother dubbed it "The Palace of the Mikado." However, the time JRS spent there was cut short and he was moved to a modest, yet elegant, townhouse on Bay State Road. Even worse, JRS was shortly thereafter removed from his seat on the board of trustees. He was shut out and would no longer have any say in Boston University's future path. That really hurt.

There had been setbacks for my dad before. Many years earlier, at his urging, Boston University had invested in a company called Seragen, which had been formed by a group of Boston University scientists whose mission was to find a cure for cancer. He believed they were developing a wonder drug that would be very effective against certain types of cancer, and as he stated at the time, "We believe we will be able to benefit mankind and make a great deal of money." The university and JRS wanted to invest even more money in the company, however, after the gubernatorial campaign in which William Weld had questioned the investment and John Silber's involvement in it, Attorney General Scott Harshbarger, as part of his political jockeying before his own failed run for governor, forced the university to draw back its financing of Seragen.

Pop always believed that the reason Seragen didn't ultimately succeed was because they lost their funding. As a result, the university lost a large sum when the price per share tanked. JRS was able to ride out the criticism over this, partly because he had accomplished the herculean task of rescuing the university from the brink of a sheer cliff of financial ruin, carried it forward to the safe and pleasant meadow of a balanced budget, and from there lifted it up to the high plateau of an endowment more than twenty times greater than when he took on the job.

When Harshbarger ran for governor in 1998, former Massachusetts State Senator Patricia McGovern opposed him for the Democratic nomination. In order to drum up interest in her candidacy, she challenged John Silber to a debate, and he was more than happy to help. As a new young lawyer at Boston University, Erika Geetter prepared John Silber for the contest and surprised everyone with her hard-hitting questions. She was a very tough debater and gave JRS a remarkably difficult time.

When Silber went on the air with McGovern, he was prepared for every issue, acquitted himself well, and was a perfect gentleman. Erika Geetter is now vice president and general counsel, as well as secretary of the board of trustees at Boston University. It is too bad Erika Geetter was not in charge of preparing JRS for debates and interviews during his 1990 run for governor. I have no doubt her efforts would have made the decisive difference.

In his first decade at Boston University, the professors twice voted to oust Silber. His work of overhauling the faculty to raise academic standards was understandably unpopular among academics whose jobs were on the line. Once, a group of vice presidents, in coordination with a few trustees, rose up against him as well. At a contentious meeting of the board of trustees, Pop was asked to leave the room while the board discussed the charges brought against him by the group of vice presidents. But Pop refused to withdraw. As he put it to the board, "My poke's on the table, and I'm not leaving." Who knows what would have happened if he had retired to the hall while they discussed his fate. He wasn't ever one to back off politely just because you asked him to. He was fond of saying, "I have a great shit detector, right here." And he would intently look you in the eye and tap his forehead. In that revolt of a few vice presidents, he was able to convince enough of the board to vote for him and keep him on.

Around the time of the Daniel Goldin fiasco, Mother and Pop were invited to a New Year's Eve Party given by a good friend of many years, David Brudnoy, a prominent radio host, a great columnist, and the best movie reviewer of his era. I was lucky to sit next to him at an event once, and I have not felt like such a brilliant conversationalist before or since. He had a way of bringing out the best in whomever he was talking to. He and Pop had admired one another professionally over many years and David Brudnoy had been very kind to Pop in the aftermath of our David's death. On the night of the party, my parents drove around Brudnoy's neighborhood but could not find the address. They went home and Pop called him. As it turned out, the party had been canceled as he was not well enough to entertain. Pop felt lucky that he hadn't heard about the cancelation because as a result, they spoke for a good while. My dad held that conversation dear, as David Brudnoy died soon after.

What more could Pop lose? The answer to that came when Mother went into the hospital for the last time. She hadn't been feeling well and they decided to keep her under observation. When Claudia and I went to see her that afternoon, she tried to talk me into taking her home. She said, "When you and Claudia go home, I think I'll just go with you." I was very torn. She clearly didn't want to stay there, and only her pride kept her from begging me.

Later, I was sorry I hadn't carried out her wish and taken her away from that ugly room, taken her home where she wanted to be. I didn't know it was the last time she would ever speak to me. A stroke in the night took her into a coma. During the next few days while she was intubated and given oxygen, we took turns sitting with her, speaking to her, and trying to get a reaction from her. Her instructions had been very clear: She did not want to be put on life support. Pop didn't make the decision to disconnect the machines on his own; he made it with the agreement and consent of all of his daughters. The doctors insisted that her brain was not functioning, but still it was horrible to stand by helplessly while they took away the tubes. Pop, Ruth, Martha, and I huddled at her bedside.

Then miraculously, after they disconnected everything, Mother went on breathing on her own. Yay, Mama! Was it possible she would beat this too? She had pulled through so many crises before; why not this time? We decided to take turns watching over her, with Pop and Ruth taking the first round. Martha and I felt ecstatic as we drove away, only to have the bottom drop out when, within an hour, the call came.

At Mother's memorial service, several of her daughters spoke, remembering different aspects of our mother. We chose some music to play during the service. Pop added songs that expressed his love for Kathryn and harkened back to their days of romance, such as Ezio Pinza singing "Some Enchanted Evening." We also played "Home on the Range."

23

Going It Alone

JRS OFTEN QUOTED CHARLES DE GAULLE, SAYING "OLD AGE IS SHIP-wreck." And yet, despite everything, he carried on as a castaway, an intellectual Robinson Crusoe, scavenging what he could and rebuilding with ingenuity.

John was surprised by how much Kathryn's death changed him. He had always been fastidious in his appearance, thinking it was his ego, his pride, that caused him to exercise, watch his weight, and spruce himself up. Even when he had worn very old clothes, veritable rags, on non-work days, they had been well laundered and crisply pressed. It came as a revelation that so much of what he did depended on Kathryn being there to see it. He would joke that he was becoming "a dirty old man."

After David's death, we had put off making a headstone because Pop had planned to sculpt a bas-relief of him for it. He had gathered together several photographs exhibiting my brother's handsome profile and taken them up to New Hampshire where his workbench and clay were ready. He tried to begin a few times but wasn't able to do it. He told me he was afraid of not quite capturing David's likeness, and also, I suspect, it hurt too much to dwell on his son's image.

Then, after Mother died, Martha and I told Pop we wanted to order a marker that commemorated both her and David. But when Pop insisted that his name should be carved in the granite as well, we gave up the idea.

It is a cliché, but nevertheless true, that work can be a lifeline. Pop took to writing and once he had the idea, his first endeavor came pouring out with ease. He wrote *Architecture of the Absurd* with a wealth of understanding gained from his lifelong interest in the subject. His premise in the book is that buildings should be functional, never degenerating into works of art that are inhospitable to the people living, working, and congregating in them. As the book shows, he clearly loved whimsical architecture, such as the works of Gaudi, where functionality is enhanced rather than lost. The pictures to illustrate the text were a bit more difficult to manage so as not to incur exorbitant fees for permission. For many of them, Pop's research assistant, Chandler Rosenberger, traveled to faraway places to take the photographs. Pop was so excited and proud when it was all assembled by the publisher and the galleys arrived for his inspection.

He took me to his office one night, the first time I had actually been inside its new location, at 73 Bay State Road. We climbed the dark stairs in the charming old townhouse and leafed through the pages together. His attitude was clearly very different toward *Architecture of the Absurd* than it had been toward the publication of *Straight Shooting* in 1989. Back then, when his first book hit the bookstores, he felt young and strong and had everything going for him. I was lucky to travel with him to Germany when the German version of *Straight Shooting* was produced. He and I walked around Berlin, stopping in each bookstore to ask if they had it. Most of them didn't, but we were hoping to drum up interest.

One evening in Heidelberg, my dad told me a strange tale that his father had once told him. It was the story of a female sea captain and her first mate, who was a German shepherd. The story had originally been narrated in German, and Pop told it to me mostly in that language after we had indulged in some strong local beer. As it happened in the story, the female sea captain and her first mate, the Schäferhund (in Germany they don't need to specify that shepherd dogs are German) had intimate relations, however the Schäferhund became so engorged that the two found it impossible to separate afterwards. As a result, the Schäferhund mauled the lady sea captain to shreds. When Johnny had first heard this story as a teenager, he realized that his father was attempting to warn him, in a roundabout clumsy way, not to be carried away by his passions or it could lead to tragic results. However, the more disturbing aspect, the image of mating between human and animal, was what lingered in his mind more dramatically. His father was trying to teach him a lesson, but what Johnny took in, with a great deal of sympathy for his revered parent, was how old-world, awkward, and out of touch his father was. It was another example of Paul G.'s dark Germanic morality, a world where lessons were always severe.

On our drive through picturesque Germany along die Romantische Strasse, the Romantic Road, thus named by our soldiers after World War II because of all the fairytale castles along it, we also stopped by to see some of Pop's favorite trees that he had been returning to look in on, for decades in some cases, like visiting with old friends. I remember we went out of our way to find one favorite, a particularly grand oak near Seebach. Pop also loved the linden trees in East Berlin, lining the boulevard called Unter den Linden, named for them. His wish was to line Commonwealth Avenue with lindens, but he was disappointed when those in charge of the plantings chose a less beautiful variety.

He was so energetic on that trip that it was really hard for me to keep up with him. Because he was then involved in so many things, *Straight Shooting* was just one interest among many. (Little did I know at the time that he was planning to run for governor of Massachusetts shortly.) When *Architecture of the Absurd* was published, it held a more significant spot in his affections. Writing the book, which came so easily to him, charged his batteries for more strenuous work ahead. Also, coming after so much loss, it proved to him that something good was possible in his desolate existence.

I say desolate, but he was not alone. He had assistants working with him on weekdays at the office or coming to the house on Carlton Street, and he had friends, as well as continuing, always, his prolific correspondence. Martha and I kept up family dinners on Saturdays and Sundays, but after Mother's death we added breakfasts as well. Pop liked to take us out on weekend mornings, taking Martha and any of her kids that wanted to go on Sundays, and me with mine on Saturdays, and when other siblings were in town they joined in. After these breakfasts, Martha or I took walks with Pop or helped him do errands. This way his weekends were quite full.

We usually drove to East Boston, where Pop had discovered a Colombian restaurant, called El Paisa, that served a breakfast buffet of delicious food to his taste. The impressive fruit offerings included mango and papaya. Pop insisted that we eat in three courses to extend the time for conversation, as was his preferred way to take meals. When Pop went up to the buffet for a bowl of fruit, our first course, he invariably took his clean fork with him so that he could stick it surreptitiously into the melon and mango chunks to see which ones were ripe. Martha and I chided him, but he continued, unembarrassed and undeterred. He only wondered why everyone didn't do the same.

Next came the main course of meats, beans with rice, and made-to-order omelets. Pop knew exactly how he liked his omelet and he gave explicit instructions for the extra crispy concoction, not too large, light on the cheese, no mushrooms, and then watched like a hawk while it was prepared. For our third course, we went back to the fruit for a bowl of berries that we ate topped with cream and sugar. All this was enjoyed with the best, rich Colombian coffee. He also became friendly with the proprietor/chef and appreciated the Colombian culture of a large proportion of the clientele. Pop loved observing and saying hello to the families. There were always young parents breakfasting with their adorable kids. He loved watching the kids, and he was glad to see that the family unit seemed to be alive and well. At these meals, Pop tended to reminisce and we often wound up laughing until we cried. Sometimes, while simply talking, he would pull out his handkerchief and wipe his eyes. JRS said that as he got older, every subject had such a wealth of background and depth of feeling that he was often brought to tears.

The next book he worked on, *Kant's Ethics*, was one he had begun while on sabbatical at Bonn University in 1960. Most of his early work had been lost or destroyed in the fire at Carlton Street, so he had to face the difficult task of rewriting those first chapters. The glassed-in sunroom that we referred to as the eating porch was where he spent many hours, the table strewn with papers, books, and his dictating machine. He had not done much of his own typing for quite a while and never took up the computer. Sadly, he was not able to work at the office allotted to him by the university because the building had no elevator, and he had developed neuropathy in his feet.

Around this time, it became clear that I needed a job. I suppose you could say I had been a "stay-at-home mom," but I never used that term and thought of it more as being in private rather than public life. I had certainly been a homemaker, always working toward creating a welcoming and enriching environment, putting together décor from secondhand finds, and in charge of keeping the books for our family budget. I marshaled my large cleaning staff (the children) while keeping to the forefront my goal of enhancing the quality of life for each individual, somehow also finding time to write and pursue my own interests. The greatest difficulty in handling this sort of enterprise is to know when your work is done, otherwise it seems like a bottomless pit. The trick is to determine your objective, decide what your job is, and then to do it.

Grandmother Jewell had once asked me what I did besides housework. I told her I was learning to ride the horses on the farm where we lived at the time. She said that was all very well, but that I ought to write. She said that one day flows into another when you are a homemaker and that it is essential to do something that stands out in your mind as an achievement for yourself. I was taken aback by her suggestion. I had been writing for many years but keeping it mostly to myself. When I lived in L.A. for ten years in my twenties, I had written a screenplay that got its share of rejections. I confided to Grandmother Jewell that I was trying to write a novel, and she heartily approved. I wouldn't share that secret with my dad until much later when I finished the first draft and asked him to read it. Among Pop's six daughters, there is a wide array of vocations, and he respected the choices of each, including mine.

When Pop lost his standing at Boston University, my husband, a brilliant and dedicated teacher who had been one of the founding lecturers of the Core Curriculum, was forced out. When his contract came up, he was not renewed. He then tried to find other employment, a rather difficult undertaking as he was sixty, quite a bit older than me. He did take on some consulting work, but this did not offer us health care, and our health insurance, on severance from the university, was expensive and would not last long.

I wasn't sure what to try. I thought I could perhaps learn to sell real estate. I liked houses and thought each one presented a unique set of possibilities, offering plenty of food for the imagination. When I talked it over with my dad, he urged me to become a teacher instead. That sounded attractive to me; I had certainly had a great deal of experience in that arena with my own children, always giving them extra reading and writing assignments in the long summer months.

As it turned out, pursuing my teaching credentials and then going on to teach elementary school was the most entertaining thing I could have done for Pop. He knew a great deal about the state of education in Massachusetts from his experience with the Chelsea schools and having headed the Massachusetts Board of Education under Bill Weld. However, this was something different because he got to see things from a teacher's perspective.

He was fascinated by every aspect of what I had to learn and then by the hoops through which I had to jump as a teacher. Some of the education impressed him immensely, but he was very frustrated with the system that inflicted on teachers so much clearly irrelevant professional development as well as the requirement of a master's degree. He seriously doubted that these produced better elementary school instructors, and he could see that the added degree cost teachers a fortune and added hours of punishing toil to their already difficult jobs. He surmised that it was something the unions and state's representatives required in order to justify hiring decisions rather than having the guts to trust their principals' choices. He believed this sort of discernment was better done on an individual basis, leaving the power with the principals, rather than getting bogged down in the search for ever higher credentials. He felt that these requirements also kept out highly qualified candidates with degrees in subjects other than education who might be interested in teaching but not in going back to college for several more years.

Shortly after I became a teacher, my husband died very suddenly and unexpectedly. How could I have faced that without my dad standing by to help in every way? For the funeral, he knew the better versions of Bible verses off the top of his head. Through it all he simply stood by, ready to help.

When everyone came to the house afterwards and I offered Pop a chair, I unthinkingly pulled out the empty chair at the head of the table, Jim's chair. Pop jumped back as if I had given him a shock of static electricity. He instantly understood the unintended implications of the gesture and the necessity of showing his proper, and truly felt, respect for Jim. You might think that's obvious. You shouldn't sit in the man's chair when he's just died. But for it to be obvious, you have to be in the moment, as Pop invariably was. He was ever alert and alive in the moment, responsive and aware of implications, never just going through the motions. That's why it was so exciting to be in his presence.

His keen sense of what was right came from his upbringing and from long years of studying ethics, but it was also instinctive with him. This sense asserted itself when it became apparent that he and his brother, Paul, could put in a claim for the property in Hamburg, Germany, that was confiscated from their Aunt Susie when she was taken away to a concentration camp by the Nazis. However, he refused to make this petition because none of the perpetrators were around to be punished. It would only be an imposition on people who currently owned the house, who had acquired it through no fault of their own. His brother, Paul, who shared the old values they inherited from their parents, agreed with this analysis of the situation, and they let go of that link to their favorite aunt.

24

The Work

THE COMPLETION OF HIS MASTERWORK, *KANT'S ETHICS*, WAS A GREAT satisfaction to Pop. It embodied the culmination of his thinking on the subject, a primary interest for his entire adult life. When the first bound copies of the book were delivered to the house, he showed me proudly how the footnotes were easily accessible at the bottom of each page, an arrangement on which he had insisted. He hated footnotes at the backs of books so that you constantly have to flip back and forth to find them. When I expressed some hesitation about even trying to read such an esoteric volume, his response was that he didn't expect me to. Its intended audience was other philosophers or at least students of philosophy.

He said that the part I would appreciate was the introduction, and we sat down together, there and then, and he read it aloud to me. He was especially pleased with the last line, about Kant looking over his shoulder as he wrote. He said that he knew it sounded ridiculously sentimental, but Kant had been the companion of his thoughts for so long he truly felt the philosopher was right there watching over his endeavor.

With this longterm goal completed, his friend Tom McCann, the author and documentary producer, encouraged my dad to dive right into another writing project. Tom was one of the first people JRS met on his arrival in Boston.

They actually met at a party, hosted by Edward Louis Bernays, the famous public relations innovator who linked the use of crowd psychology and propaganda techniques with the communication of a public image for individual clients and followers. It fascinates me that Pop was invited to a social gathering by this man from whom he could have learned so much about public manipulation, but with his way of facing the world so juxtaposed against façade, my dad could not benefit from Bernays's methods.

Tom recalls John "looking like an outsider, just standing back getting the lay of the land," at that party. Pop had, just that day, signed his contract with Boston University, and he didn't know anyone yet. He had also signed a lease on an apartment at Emerson Place, advertised with a large sign at the end of Storrow Drive, near North Station, stating, "If You Lived Here, You'd Be Home Now." Pop lived there for several months, until the end of the school year, when the rest of the family joined him in Boston.

Pop would not be an "outsider" for long. He loved Boston, not so much the area around Emerson Place, but the old architecture of the Back Bay and Brookline, or the North End and the South End. He loved to walk the beautiful streets, illuminated by antique streetlamps, and soak in the layers of history. Pop made Boston our home and never looked back.

On the night of Bernays's party, JRS asked his new acquaintance, "When are they going to bring out the food?"

"Oh you won't get any food at a Cambridge cocktail party," Tom informed him.

I'm sure Pop was already planning his own contribution to Boston society. For one thing, he and Kathryn would always serve delicious food with the drinks at their parties, not just "tidbits and dabs of cheese." He and Tom left the party and found a meal at the old Wursthaus in Harvard Square. Pop came to realize that Tom was someone he could trust, someone to go in the trenches with, someone who would be ready to go over the top with a knife between his teeth.

Over the years they often worked together on committees at the Algonquin Club. At Arthur Metcalf's suggestion, Pop had, on his arrival in Boston, joined the Algonquin, located in a grand old building on Commonwealth Avenue.

The Algonquin Club was one of the first Boston clubs to accept female members, and yet, the club was still old-fashioned. There was a strict dress code. If a man arrived not wearing a tie, he was offered one to borrow so that he could enter. My husband suffered the embarrassment of having to wear a borrowed tie over the turtleneck he was wearing one time in the late 1980s.

When it was time to elect a new president of the club in 1995, Tom pointed out to my dad that it was really Katherine McAvoy's turn. A philanthropist who had been a club member for many years, she had served on almost every committee, but the club had never had a female president. Pop agreed but said there wasn't enough time to make it happen that year.

Pop backed his good friend Jim Howell, who was in the running to be the next president. Jim was a great guy and a convivial club member, but he was not ideal president-of-the-club material. For one thing, he sometimes drank a bit too much before club business meetings. Pop had guessed how it would be and saw his friend's tenure as a prelude for a different sort of candidate.

When it came time to choose the next president, Pop could back Katherine McAvoy and get Arthur Metcalf and others to sign on as well. As my dad explained it, "Arthur didn't agree, and he didn't like electing the first woman for the job, but he could see that supporting her for president was the right thing to do."

After the publication of *Kant's Ethics*, Tom suggested that JRS assemble a book of his best speeches. The trouble was that nobody really wants to publish a book of speeches, so the goal was to turn the speeches into chapters by adding context to each one, where and when it was given, and what was going on in the world at the time that prompted the ideas.

The resulting book, *Seeking the North Star*, has as its first chapter "The Pollution of Time," Pop's first speech at Boston University, delivered at his inauguration as president. The final chapter was a new speech he meant for the launch of the book hosted by the Consular Corps and the Algonquin Club. Unfortunately, when the day came, he was not well enough to deliver that speech, and the event was canceled. Brian Jorgensen, his colleague of many years, then took on the task of seeing the book through to publication.

JRS was beset with several maladies during these years. When asked how he felt, his standard reply was, "Out of warranty." Neuropathy in his feet curtailed his ability to walk comfortably, cutting him off from one of his greatest pleasures. His way of seeing and understanding any city had always been to walk its streets, so having this method of getting around seriously limited was punishment indeed. He also had developed a blood disorder that he suspected had its origins in his use of pesticides on the trees he loved. He could remember, as a young man, spraying the chemicals high into the branches and feeling it, carried by the wind, raining down on him. Why hadn't he realized that was bad for him? It made him feel like an idiot to think about how oblivious he had been.

Just as it had been with Mother, a fall brought everything down to a different level. On a rainy day, after the funeral of Governor King at the State House, Pop slipped on the marble steps, worn smooth with age, smashing his shoulders and pelvis. One shoulder required very delicate surgery. The way Pop described it made it sound like his body parts were barely holding together and that the surgeon could hardly find any sinew to which his shoulder could be reattached. It was clear he would not be able to use his hand for some time while his arm healed. The other shoulder was also injured, fragile, and sore.

He was overcome by a sense of desperation when realizing he could not even tend to himself at all during this recovery. He needed around-the-clock attention, but he dreaded being confined in a rehab hospital. Martha ordered a special chair for him that was extra cushioned and also reclined. Pop could sleep in this chair rather than trying to get in and out of bed, and that was a great help. However, he still needed someone to be there twenty-four hours a day. Martha started researching what services were available, and then Charles came to the rescue. He flew to Boston to take care of Pop and be his companion for several weeks. This was a very difficult job because most of Pop's body was in pain and he was very weak.

To assist him as he walked or to help him move from the chair to another location, it was necessary to take hold of Pop around the waist. He was in constant fear that someone, with the best intentions, would grab him by the arm to help him up, and not only hurt like hell, but rip his shoulder loose again. He and Charles spent their time watching movies and the History Channel, until finally Pop was ready for the next stage, more action and exercise. Charles initiated a program called "restaurant therapy" that Martha and I gladly participated in. As a way of getting Pop to leave the house and get used to going places, we all went out to lunch several days a week. There was a lot of laughter and fun in these outings and it helped Pop make the transition to rejoining the active world. Unfortunately, Charles couldn't stay forever; he had his own family in Arkansas to get back to.

This diminished father, more frail than I imagined he could be, took some getting used to. The only time I could remember his being really ill before was when he came down with sarcoidosis a year or so after coming to Boston University. I remember the strangeness of entering his hospital room and finding him there, docilely watching *Sesame Street* on television. This was the seventies, when *Sesame Street* was still fairly new. After his fall, our dynamo parent wasn't mentally docile, but he was a less active, less capable man. I was beginning to understand that despite what I had believed all my life, my father was not always able to do everything.

Out of exasperation, he would cry out in frustration if something in the refrigerator was tied shut or put in a small ziplock bag and he couldn't get it open, so that he had to resort finally to cutting it open with a knife. For the first time, I saw his stub as an actual disability.

Leslie Epstein, the novelist and a colleague at Boston University, as well as the father of Theo Epstein, one-time Red Sox GM, invited him to join a regular poker game. He was pleased to be invited and attended a few times. He even hosted the group once but felt bad about not playing well. He told me he wished they would just meet to talk. He said he didn't like doing something badly and he did not play cards enough in his life to do it well. The players in the group were quite advanced, and he didn't want to ruin their game.

Martha took charge of all his medications, learning their names and properties, and sorting them out each week into morning and evening dispensers. She also did most of the preparation of meals, stocking Pop's refrigerator with choices. Two of her college student sons, John David and Brendan, moved into the Carlton Street house so their grandfather would not be entirely alone. The large rambling place no longer had full-time caretakers.

Pedro and Walter, from the university Buildings and Grounds Department, looked in on their rounds of the nearby properties and made sure the heat and so forth were working properly, and one maid, Maria, came a few days a week. This was very different from the full-time staff that had formerly maintained the house in glowing perfection. Pop developed a cordial rapport with Maria, but this never approached his relationship with her predecessor, the longtime housekeeper at the Carlton Street house, Katie Cadogan. Her given name was Keiko, but she went by Katie, as she had met and married a Boston Irishman in the aftermath of World War II. JRS, and all of us, admired her fastidious nature and competence and appreciated the cheerful interest she took in our objectives. He and Katie had a playful competition through the years over the maintenance of several large potted plants. His green thumb with trees did not extend to this realm. Katie would let Pop tend to a plant up to the point where it was about to expire, and then, when he was ready to discard it, she would take over and slowly but surely bring it back to full, luxuriant flower.

With only himself and the two young men rattling around in the house, Pop drew up an elaborate chart to keep in the kitchen, on which he and his grandsons could sign in, sign out, and leave comments for each other. This gave each of them the freedom to go about their own business in the large house while still, at a moment's notice, being able to see who was in or out. All of the grandchildren liked to sign in on the chart as well and write notes or draw pictures on it for their Grandaddy when they came to Carlton Street.

His next challenge was an increasing failure of the kidneys that required dialysis. Once again, Martha took charge of understanding all the medical issues. As always, Pop frequently consulted with his in-family medical expert, albeit a veterinarian, Alexandra. Martha regularly prepared Pop for his dialysis, made sure that his pillows, books, and other necessities were in his bag, and usually transported him there and back. Sometimes, other visiting siblings accompanied Pop on these expeditions, sitting with him and reading to him, still one of his greatest pleasures. Brian Jorgensen on occasion went along and read to him from *Team of Rivals*. Jennifer Horgan and Kelly O'Connor sometimes sat with him and worked on correspondence.

I only took him for these treatments a few times, and when I did, it was terribly difficult to stand by and watch him writhing in pain. Looking around at the other patients, it was clear that some people did not have such a difficult time. His tiny, shrunken veins were hard to find and the technicians had to stab him again and again.

Early one morning, I arrived at the Carlton Street house to prepare Pop for dialysis and found him sprawled on the floor. He was not wearing his emergency call button, and his phone was up on the table where he couldn't reach it. He had been lying on the floor for several hours after falling in the night. I rushed to his side, crying out, but he was ready for me and immediately started giving sharp, precise orders, "Listen to me, Rachel. Do not call an ambulance. Call Martha and find Pedro and Walter to help me up." He had been lying there, as mentally sharp and tenacious as ever, planning his strategy, determined not to be taken to an emergency room.

With great difficulty, Walter, Pedro, Martha, and I got Pop back into his chair, and then got him out of his pajamas and into his clothes. Dialysis had to be canceled, put off for another day. When Martha succeeded in getting Pop's orthopedic specialist on the phone, he said we could come right over, so somehow, Pedro and Walter managed to get Pop out of the house and into the car, and we all set off to see the doctor. This maneuvering was difficult because it was not possible to hold him by his delicate, painful arms. When we arrived at the medical complex and got out of the car, we were all standing around waiting for someone to bring a wheelchair for Pop. Pedro took that opportunity to say, very earnestly to JRS, "Someday, President Silber, I'm going to tell my grandchildren," and he paused, to gather his thoughts before continuing, "that I touched John Silber's butt."

Of course, that broke us all up. The whole excursion, from that moment, took on a lighthearted air. Yes, Pop was in bad shape, and yes, if Martha and I had been willing to do what we thought was best and overrule our dad's wishes, we would have checked him into the hospital. As it turned out, I will always remember the way the whole gang of us flouted conventional wisdom that day. It seemed like a fine caper, like playing hooky, an event to be relished at the time and cherished in retrospect.

25

Final Challenges

Pop's KIDNEY FAILURE GOT DRAMATICALLY WORSE; THE DIALYSIS WAS barely able to keep him going. Months before, the medical team had offered him a kidney transplant, but Pop didn't let us cling to that hope for a moment. He turned them down outright, refusing to consider taking a kidney that could go to one of the many young people who needed it as badly as he did. I asked, "What about your friend, the one who was always claiming to have three kidneys and swearing, after a few glasses of wine, to be ready to give one to any of your kids or grandkids who might need one someday? Why don't you call him and ask if he'd like to give you one?" But Pop just laughed, seemingly amused by the memory of that grandiose offer, then shaking his head, he said, "No, no, that wouldn't be right."

A meeting was called to discuss Pop's options. His doctors were there and all of his children attended either in person or by speakerphone. I'm sure the meeting was really just for our benefit. Pop posed the relevant questions to the medical team so that we could hear the answers. He asked something like, "Can I get better or will I continue to get less and less benefit from the dialysis?" and, "If I stop the treatment, is there any way that decision can be considered a form of suicide?"

The doctors confirmed for us what Pop had already determined for himself. He would not get better. The effectiveness of the dialysis would only decline. Forgoing further dialysis could not be considered tantamount to committing suicide.

I wanted him to keep up the effort a while longer. I had confidence in his mental strength. I believed if he willed it, he could hang on. I remembered Pop, only a few years earlier, quoting Dylan Thomas when he and I had gone to visit his dying friend, Dick Thissen, in the hospital.

Do not go gentle into that good night,
Old age should burn and rave at close of day;
Rage, rage against the dying of the light.

He had wanted more time with his friend. Not for any great project, just for another convivial evening. Time for conversation, time for feasting and merrymaking. I wanted Pop to hang on for the same reasons. I wanted him to be there so I could talk to him, enjoy his company, and look into his wise, loving eyes. I wasn't ready to let go.

But he was too tired, and he couldn't rage on. It was clear he had been looking ahead, preparing the way for a long time. On Thanksgiving almost a year before, the family had gathered at the Carlton Street house. Pop, already weak and in pain, took that opportunity, while all his children were congregated in one place and with the executor of his will, Joe Mercurio, present, to read his will. Because he read the will in person, with all of us there, he was able to answer our questions and resolve any misunderstandings, so there would be no surprises later.

At the same time, he also divided among us the many works of art he had collected over the years. On the numbered card for each, there was a description and photograph of the artwork. We drew lots to determine our place in the lineup, and then, sitting around the dining room table, we began several rounds of making choices. He said we could go ahead and take the works then, but most of us didn't take him up on that. Later, when the time did come, there were no disputed memories of what went to whom because our choices had been noted and we each had the cards for the works we had chosen.

Several friends stopped by to see him and he wrote letters to a few others, to say goodbye. He was touchingly thoughtful at the end. He wanted to make sure all of us would be alright.

One day he asked Martha, "What ever happened to Britney Spears?" A few years earlier, when she had had her nervous breakdown and shaved off all her hair, Pop had felt tremendous sympathy for her and had furiously wondered where her parents were. He was gratified when Martha was able to tell him that Britney had gotten her life and career back on track and seemed happy and relatively healthy at the time. I can't guess what he would think about the controversy over Britney's conservatorship. Would he find that parental control can go too far, and that an adult needs to have freedom, even the freedom to fail? One of the saddest things is not being able to hear his reaction to things as they happen. I can sometimes guess what he'd think, but I can never ask him.

The only project of his own that Pop was still concerned about was his last book, *Seeking the North Star*. Its publication date was looming, and he was hoping his friend, Tom Wolfe, would write a foreword for it. Tom had another project he was occupied with and Pop was worried that he might not be able to do the foreword in time.

Simple care, like bathing, was an ongoing problem because Pop was in such terrible pain. We were lucky, at last, to find a woman who was able to do the job without hurting Pop too much. She was a large woman with a motherly gentleness, and Pop said he felt she bathed him just like he was her little baby. Being so fastidious all his life, it was a great comfort to be sweet smelling and clean in fresh pajamas.

There wasn't much time after Pop stopped going to dialysis, and there was very little any of us could do for him. I made him a bouilla-baisse, something easy to eat, and one of his favorite meals. I also made some oatmeal cookies. Pop loved cookies and often pretended to be the Cookie Monster, calling out for a "Coookieee," in a monster growl. Martha usually made the oatmeal cookies he liked to eat with his first cup of coffee each day. I don't usually bake cookies. Correction: as my kids know, I never bake cookies. I consider them too labor intensive compared to other desserts like cakes or brownies. But Martha and I both made some of those oatmeal and raisin cookies he liked for him in the last days.

Then, an email came from Tom Wolfe. He was on the project and he attached the beginning of his foreword. Pop was so pleased when I read him the first few paragraphs:

> I pledge you my word, it came popping out of my mouth just like that, as if The Force had commandeered my voice box to make an announcement.
>
> This was the evening of October 16, 2008, nineteen days before the presidential election, Barack Obama vs.

John McCain, a matter of minus-ten interest to me at that moment. I was here in Chicago for a Chicago Public Library book program...holding forth, as requested, upon a book about the original Mercury astronauts and their adventures half a century ago, *The Right Stuff*.

No sooner had I left the rostrum than an ace blogcaster for the online *Huffington Post*, Greg Boose, appeared: "Do you think that either of these candidates have 'the right stuff'?'"

Without a moment of reflection, without even a Well... or an Ummmm...my voice box said, "I'm voting for John Silber, a write-in vote. He was President of Boston University—not College—and he almost won the governorship of Massachusetts in 1990. He's a Democrat, but no matter what, he's like Epictetus, the Stoic. He cannot assent to what he knows is wrong. He cannot disagree with what he knows is right."

Pop was content. He felt satisfied that his book was in good hands and that it would be complete.

The day after that, I found him tucked in bed like a sleepy little boy. He had had another bath, and his hair was clean and combed. He seemed too tired to speak. I sat on the edge of the bed beside him and he looked up at me and said, "I love looking at your face." And I said, "I love looking at yours."

Judith looked in on him a little later. She found him lying very still, keeping his eyes closed, but she could tell he wasn't asleep. Noticing that his lips were a bit chapped, Judith found a ChapStick and rubbed it on them. He jerked his eyes open and pulled away, then went back to lying very still with his eyes closed. She said that it seemed like he was holding himself alert, waiting for death. She felt he didn't want to fall asleep and miss it. It would be a final discovery for him to see what death was like.

Just as Pop felt Immanuel Kant looking over his shoulder as he wrote, I have sometimes felt my dad looking over mine. I can just hear him asking me, "Why are you writing so much about my ailments? Why are you even mentioning them?" It's very simple. I'm writing about them because of how well he carried his burdens. He carried them with honor, with dignity, and without complaint. I am so proud of the way he faced every adversity and met every challenge. He was a man of principle to the end. At crunch time, his principles held because he believed in them. He was content and never hesitated before doing the right thing.

26

Tribute

WHEN POP DIED, HE COULDN'T GO TO WATERMAN'S IN KENMORE Square, where David and Mother had been prepared for burial, because it was no longer there. Caroline, my youngest sister, and I set out to see him at an unfamiliar establishment in Brookline, but the spot turned out to be familiar after all. It was across the street from the Brookline Library, where I used to study during high school. The spot where I parked may have been the exact spot where I once got a parking ticket when I stayed too long at the library with several friends, including Peggy Dalzell, a perfect companion as it turned out, when the car had a citation on our return to it.

I remember, we scampered down the sidewalk toward the police station where Peggy spotted her father getting out of the passenger side of a police car and preparing to enter the building. She called to him and then when we drew near she very charmingly begged him to take care of the ticket. I was embarrassed and didn't want him to think I expected the favor, but the police chief didn't seem to be taken aback and he obviously adored his lovely daughter.

Not having been to this part of Brookline in a while, it brought back floods of memory from when we first arrived in the Boston area and Judith and I enrolled at The High School. We thought the name very farcical as it seemed to have an awfully high opinion of itself as the ultimate high school. There was more amusement when we learned that the country club in Brookline had a similar case of self-importance, calling itself The Country Club. Alexandra, Martha, and Laura Ruth had entered Lawrence Elementary, where Laura became Ruth, and little Caroline had begun nursery school.

Pop was laid out in a coffin in a small sitting room area. He looked very sweet, and I could imagine him tucked in bed as a boy, waiting patiently for his parents to come say goodnight and hear his prayers. The only detail discordant with this image was his pair of large, owlish reading glasses. I asked the attendant why he was wearing them and was told that many people aren't recognizable without the glasses that they usually wore in life.

This wasn't true of our dad. Besides being eminently recognizable, he never wore glasses except for reading or fine work of some kind, so I took them off and put them in my pocket. That was better.

Caroline and I sat and reminisced. As the older sibling, I am used to thinking I am the one taking care of others, but I felt that evening that my youngest sister was the one supporting me, staying patiently as long as I wanted.

I think when Pop died, my sisters and I all felt we wanted to express what he meant to us. It is hard to know what you can do for someone who has given you so much, made life so rich with meaning, and loved you. Later that night, I wrote a tribute to him that I subsequently read at his funeral. Several of my sisters wrote eulogies as well. Here is mine:

Who Will Speak for Him

Over the years, Pop has been asked to speak at the funerals of many people, too many friends. I don't think there is anyone better at considering a person's life, finding the essence of that individual, and honoring it. I have sometimes wondered, "Who on earth could speak for Pop?" I can't do it as he would, but I will tell you some things I've seen and heard from him.

From his earliest years, my father was interested in the individual. When he was about three or four, at the beginning of the Depression, when Pop's father still worked and the family lived in a very nice house, he and his brother Paul were playing one day at the back of their yard. They climbed up the fence and saw a terrible looking man sorting through the trash cans in the alley.

My father, with some trepidation asked him, "What are you?" to which the man replied forcefully, "I'm a human being!" This made a great impression on young Johnny— perhaps the beginning of his life as a philosopher.

However, for quite a long time he didn't know what he wanted to be. He tried several avenues, not lightly as a dabbler, but diving in with his whole heart and being. Mother was there for many of these explorations, the two having married when they were twenty.

For a time he was a musician, playing the trumpet. As an artist, drawing, painting, and especially sculpting, he worked on the façades of several of his architect father's buildings. Never less than forthright, he has stated that he was a better sculptor than his father. But he thought, "Not good enough."

Then, as he has said, he "got the religious bug," which took him to Yale Divinity School, where he gave sermons and led a church choir, as choir director. But, after a while, as he put it, "I got that monkey off my back" when he made the move to philosophy.

David and I were born during those years, and as soon as Pop had his PhD, he and mother packed us up and he began his work at the University of Texas.

As a child, in Austin, I was very aware of his love of trees. I remember the tall wavy sycamores and blossoming redbud trees. He also bought a fig tree from a local nursery. Figs were one of his great loves. The trees all began very small, less than three feet, but under his care they grew very quickly.

In 1959 and 60, we lived in Germany, while Pop studied at Bonn University. Rather than living in a tiny city apartment, my father rented a sizeable one with a fenced backyard in the nearby village of Pech. He put us in German schools in Bad Godesberg at which no one spoke English. Because of this we all speedily learned to speak German fluently. Most mornings when he drove us into town for school, he would pick up neighbors waiting at the bus stop and drive them in too. He was always so interested in what people thought and sometimes he would ask very pointed questions about what happened during the war, and how much they knew about it at the time. He was never one to back off from an uncomfortable subject.

During that year, we traveled around Germany, Italy, France, and England. Our grandmotherly neighbor, Frau Anderseck, came along to help herd all of us. My sisters and I have sometimes tried to figure out how three adults and four children fit into that Volkswagen Beetle.

When Pop took another sabbatical, in 1963, we lived in London. This time, we children were enrolled in British schools and acquired British accents. I remember picking blackberries on Hampstead Heath and a trip to Oxford to see a twilight production of *A Midsummer Night's Dream*, performed outside among the real fireflies. On jaunts like this, we took along wonderful picnic lunches and were often accompanied by the philosopher, John Findlay, and his wife Aileen.

Pop could also make very unlikely friends. One evening at the nearby pub, he met a thief named Thomas. He knew right away Thomas was a thief because he tried to sell Pop a brand new camera for a very low price. Pop didn't buy the camera, but he brought Thomas home to dinner on several occasions and they had some absorbing conversations.

My father even let Thomas take us children to the pictures, *The Son of Captain Blood* as I recall. Pop has marveled in recent years that he allowed this relative stranger to take us out on the town, but I believe he had sized up Thomas' character very well. Thomas was a thief, but he was also a thoroughly decent human being.

Pop accomplished so much in his life. His devotion to Boston University was boundless. It was the great work of his life to nurture and care for it and for all the people who made it.

From the earliest stage of his career, he was passionately interested in the education of young children, from working on the bipartisan commission that established Head Start to his work with the Chelsea Schools where there is now a Center for Early Education in his name.

In the Barbara Smith controversy at the University of Texas in 1957, he forcefully protested when she was removed from a student opera because of her race. This, at a time when he had no tenure and his job was on the line.

He also worked as chairman of the Texas Society to Abolish Capital Punishment, a cause he never wavered from.

He was a marvelous sculptor. His bas-relief of Arthur Metcalf and the one of Elie Wiesel are very true to life, though Arthur did ask Pop to spare him a few years under the chin.

He waged a valiant campaign for governor, missing by a narrow margin. He would have been a great governor for Massachusetts.

He has written several books, *Straight Shooting* came first, followed by my favorite, *Architecture of the Absurd*. His next book, *Kant's Ethics*, is the culmination of fifty years of study, and his final book, a collection of essays, is titled *Seeking the North Star*.

These, and more that I have not mentioned, are great achievements for one life. But in his last days, Pop wasn't dwelling on them. He was remembering my mother—things she said, her quick wit that so delighted him. He was remembering his children and friends, things they had done or said, things he had shared with them.

When I saw him on the morning of his dying, he was lying in bed, but he had his shoulders squared, his chin jutting forward, his brow calm. He looked ready to face anything.

27

The End of an Era

THE CARLTON STREET HOUSE HAS STOOD EMPTY SINCE POP'S PASS-
ing. We heard that it was bought by Boston Children's Hospital to be
used as a sort of haven where families could stay when one of their
children was hospitalized. My sisters and I were so pleased to hear of
this and hoped to volunteer there someday. We could picture ourselves
in the kitchen cooking breakfast for the families, but that plan for the
house hasn't come about. As rumor has it, the zoning for the project fell
through. So the great house has been sitting empty with black plastic
in the windows. It is now on the market again, but it seems to be dete-
riorating. The shutters are broken and some of them hang crookedly.

I look around to see what remains of Pop's tremendous spirit.
Thankfully, he spent his final years industriously finishing his books. I
have reread the introduction to *Kant's Ethics*, and it makes me smile to
remember him reading it aloud to me as if I were a child. I have also
reread *Architecture of the Absurd* and will read it many times more as
it is so much fun. His understanding of what good architecture must
embrace in order to be amenable to human experience is a value that
is flouted too often. When I see positive or negative examples of this,
I so wish I could tell him about them.

Perhaps the greatest gift is his final book, *Seeking the North Star*,
published after his death. It is a treasure trove of insights into the
world we inhabit. I so appreciate having the opportunity to explore his
well-formed thoughts and to have this artifact of his impressive life
of the mind. In the essay, "Procedure or Dogma: The Core of Liberalism," quoted extensively in this book, Pop advocates strongly for the
protection of our right to free speech. This right is threatened today,
especially on college campuses, by those who would silence the voices
of those with opposing beliefs.

One thing I would recommend to readers is that they read the
last chapter first. Titled "The Choices Are Ours," it was planned as

a speech to launch the publication of the book and is still eminently relevant, addressing today's pressing issues. In it he speaks directly to those he leaves behind, explicitly elucidating his concerns and also offering encouragement.

I wish Pop had also modeled or drawn a portrait of himself. Some photographs capture him accurately, but I am not entirely satisfied with any of the busts or paintings. Ray Kinstler painted the official Boston University portrait of him. JRS and Kinstler were great friends and admired one another's work tremendously. The only comment I heard Pop make about the verisimilitude of the official portrait was that a friend of his daughter, Caroline, saw it on display in New York City and recognized him immediately, so he concluded that it must look like him. It is a fine painting that does capture something of the benevolent attitude he evinced as President Silber when wearing his ceremonial robes at commencement, but the face doesn't really look like him. It might be a brother. You can see the family resemblance. It just isn't quite John Silber.

Another great artist and friend, Neil Welliver, painted an impressive portrait of him. In it he is seated before a beautiful, intricate tapestry, but his eyes glower from a gray face, deeply wrinkled with intense gloom. Pop was horrified and insulted when he saw it. He and Welliver wrote letters back and forth to one another about it. It was never hung publicly, but JRS and he remained friends, and the work was not destroyed. Pop kept it at his office, where we found it after he died.

Then the question was: What to do with it? I thought I might create a Naughty Room at my house and hang it there. Then anytime someone misbehaved they could be sent to that room and have Grandaddy scowl at them for a while. Finally, Martha decided to keep it at her house, where it commands a place of honor in her dining room. Surprisingly, we have all become rather fond of the scowling old man.

When I went with Pop to Marc Mellon's studio to see his bust of my dad, I was once again not entirely pleased. It certainly captured my dad's strength, but not the fineness of his looks and character. As I told my dad at the time, I wish he had sculpted a self-portrait. When I observe the subtlety with which he captured the features, mien, and personality of Arthur Metcalf, Elie Wiesel, and his old friend Virgil Wolfenberg, I am convinced he could have done a splendid bust of himself. Or, more likely, a bas-relief, as he was always most fascinated by profiles, forever drawing them at odd moments on any type of surface, a sheet of scrap paper, or a napkin at a restaurant.

I was once put on the spot when Arthur Metcalf painted a portrait of my dad and then asked me what I thought of it. I had studied the oil painting where it had been hung for a while over the fireplace in the living room at Carlton Street, trying to grasp why it failed to capture his likeness. The face was narrower than it should have been and the eyes too close together. It looked a little like Mitt Romney crossed with Randolph Scott. Floundering for something to say I blurted out, "It's not quite the face of the sweetie pie I know and love." This satisfied Arthur and he laughed, "No, no. It's not the face of a sweetie pie."

I am fond of a drawing in charcoal, signed *C. A. Tierney*. It was done in 1978, and I love to look at it because it captures quite well Pop's characteristic pensive look. The thoughtful guy in this picture, with so much longing in his heart, is who my dad truly was. He always had big dreams and high ideals. He never lost them even as he grew older and became less confident of a positive outcome. In the preface to *Seeking the North Star*, he says, "…although I remain an intellectual pessimist, I am at the same time a congenital optimist." His judicious intellect is the counterpoise to his positive, hopeful heart.

Now, the question is: What will become of Pop's papers, memorabilia, speeches, recordings? Shortly after he died, his staff at the Bay State Road townhouse office sent the material that was deemed to be official university business (budgets, interoffice memos, official letters, longterm planning, minutes of trustee meetings, etc.) directly to the archive storage facility. Everything else (his prolific correspondence, the annotated drafts of his speeches, memorabilia, honors, and awards, etc.) were sent to the house on Carlton Street where Martha and I began the difficult task of sorting through all of it.

Then, we met at the university with Director Vita Paladino, the assistant directors, and staff of the Howard Gotlieb Archival Research Center at the Boston University Library where we were told they had great plans for the material. They said the John Silber collection would be the largest in the library's special collection and that parts of it would be prominently displayed from time to time.

They also said that a website would be created that would offer the experience of watching and listening to John Silber's speeches so that those who had not been fortunate enough to see him in person could experience the excitement of hearing him speak.

Luckily, Pop had often kept both sides of his correspondence, the letters written to him as well as copies of the letters he had written. This correspondence would give insight into the evolution of his thoughts and relationships.

Martha and I were very pleased with these initial plans and we signed an agreement with the university so that the material could be picked up by staff from the university and the task of sorting and inventorying the collection could get underway.

The university has held the John Silber collection for eight years. The inventory has not been completed, so we have not been able to finalize the gift of the collection to Boston University. It is not clear what the university's plans are for the collection; what is clear is that they are vastly different from what was described ten years ago when Pop passed away.

The future of the Howard Gotlieb Archival Research Center is also uncertain; for now, it no longer has a director and has been subordinated under the head of the library.

After Pop's death, the university had a memorial service. It was a fine event and well-meant, but like the portraits of Pop, it didn't quite capture him. Some of the speakers made him sound like a rather bluff and boorish Texan, without seeming to realize how sincerely John Silber felt he was not just a Texan anymore. He had made Boston his home. Even back when he still lived in Texas, he was a complicated, deeply cultured, and learned man. At any rate, the image of a coarse, blustering Texan is a false stereotype. Gentlemanly manners are highly prized and cultivated there. Pop's parents made sure he learned those gentle manners, but from the earliest age he was also more forthright, outspoken, and forceful than would be consistent with perfect politeness. Brought up with old-world manners, JRS always cut through them with his intense, unstoppable search for truth.

In true institutional form, the philosophy department at Boston University was represented at the memorial service by its chairman, a fine speaker, but she had never even met John Silber. My sister, Martha, her son, Joseph, as well as Joe Mercurio, and several friends and previous students saved the day by offering personal and heartfelt tributes.

The best memorials for John Silber took place while he was still alive and able to enjoy them. He was so delighted when the city of Boston and its mayor, Tom Menino, took Sherborn Street at the heart of Boston University, and renamed it Silber Way. In his last years, he loved driving by and noting the name. It gave him a kick. As Mayor Menino reminisced about it:

> I was trying to think of some way to show the City's appreciation to John in a durable, lasting manner. It came on me that naming a street Silber Way was a highly appropriate gesture. Naturally, the joke about Silber Way or the Highway quickly caught on, but given the way John transformed a small commuting school into a national powerhouse of learning and research, let me tell you: given a choice I would always take Silber's way.
>
> At the dedication ceremony John was thoroughly gracious and he mentioned that I was up for re-election. He then offered to endorse me or, if it helped more, he offered to endorse my opponent. Anything to get me re-elected. That was my friend John Silber.

In 2007, at a magnificent gala celebration that was held in his honor, JRS described himself as Tom Sawyer enjoying his own funeral. He said to the crowd, "While I can't claim to be terribly modest, I am modest enough to be embarrassed." It was a huge event with almost a thousand people attending. I have never seen so many people. Speakers ranged from the worlds of the academy to politics, the arts and literature to sports and business. He was greatly honored that evening, but each speech was also a testimony of love and friendship. It was a tremendous warmhearted outpouring.

The evening began on an affectionate note with opening remarks by Trustee and Gala Committee Chairman Fred Chicos remembering the role JRS played in his life when his own father died and appreciating him for his encouragement and sense of humor. President Robert Brown expressed his appreciation for the years that Boston University was "infused with a sense of urgency" on John Silber's watch. Mayor Tom Menino, Tom Wolfe, super-attorney Bob Popeo, soprano Phyllis Curtin, and dozens more recounted amusing stories and heaped heartfelt praise on John Silber.

So many wanted to be involved that the planning committee swelled to one hundred and sixteen members, and there were another fifty-one honorary co-chairmen.

When Pop died, it was a relief for my siblings and me to finally feel free to choose a headstone for Mother and David, since we could now add Pop's name as well. Our dad had also chosen an epitaph for himself. It was a line from a poem he wrote in 1946 that had been inspirational to him all his adult life: "A sparrow would as eagle fly." It expressed perfectly how he saw himself. He was confident that he could accomplish great things, but he never mistook himself for a giant among men. He had a surprisingly humble view of himself and felt that it was only by force of will and dedication that he was able to accomplish so much.

Martha has often seen a sparrow on her porch that makes her think of our dad. I find a great variety of sparrows congregating around my house. Many of them are quite round and fluffy, but sometimes a rather lean sparrow separates himself from the flock and hops forward—standing up very straight on his little twig legs, with his wings tucked behind, as if he is pulling his shoulders back, exhibiting perfect posture. And holding his head just so, the little sparrow seems to give me a particularly friendly and intelligent look. I get the feeling Pop is saying hello.

Top: When Mother wore heels, she was sometimes a bit taller than Pop. Silber Family Photos. *Bottom:* My parents loved to dance. On trips together they would be sure to find a place that had a good band so they could enjoy "cutting the rug." Boston University Photography.

Top: Prince Edward, Diana Rigg, and JRS at Boston University. Prince Edward was honored with the Bette Davis Achievement Award for his documentary work, September 2000. *Bottom:* Robert Brustein, founder of the American Repertory Theater, Elie Wiesel, and JRS looking at an exhibit at the opening of the Robert Brustein Collection at the Gotlieb Center at Boston University.
Allan Dines Photography.

Top: JRS and Rose Girouard had a way of adding some fun to events. Here President Silber pretends he is inspecting the troops. *Bottom:* JRS and Kathryn with architect and friend Scott Simpson at the event to introduce the ill-fated, almost-president Daniel Goldin to the Boston University community in the fall of 2003. It was the first event my mother attended after being very unwell. Allan Dines Photography.

Top: President Silber walking with author Tom Wolfe after the Boston University Commencement on Nickerson Field on May 21, 2000, at which JRS presented Wolfe with a splendid white commencement gown, trimmed in BU scarlet velvet. Photo by Albert L'Etoile for Boston University Photography.
Bottom: President Silber with Boston Mayor Thomas Menino at Harry Agganis Way Day on November 11, 1995.
Photo by Kalman Zabarsky for Boston University Photography.

Dear John,

If you would like independent verification of the fidelity of the depiction below, I can provide it in the person of SUZANNE CUTLER, who was there as I walked onto DELTA SHUTTLE FLIGHT 4081

First page of the letter Tom Wolfe wrote to JRS after the 2000 Commencement. Tom illustrated his letter with a drawing of himself wearing his new commencement robes home on the plane. John Silber Collection.

JRS making a mold for casting his clay bas-relief of Arthur Metcalf in bronze. Boston University Photography.

JRS with his bas-relief of Arthur Metcalf cast in bronze.
Boston University Photography.

Top: Virgil Wolfenberg posing with the bust of him sculpted by JRS. In this picture you can see why Ampee called Virgil "The Sheik." Silber Family Photos.
Bottom: The poster JRS made for the first performance of Bill Arrowsmith's translation of Aristophanes' *The Birds*, with his drawing of Bill as Pan.
Photo by J. C. Johnson.

Top: Portrait of JRS in oil, by Arthur Metcalf. Arthur got the eyes too close together. I thought it looked like a cross between Mitt Romney and Randolph Scott. *Bottom:* JRS with Bill Arrowsmith. Boston University Photography.

President John Silber having his portrait painted by Ray Kinstler at 147 Bay State Road, September 1995.
Photos by Kalman Zabarsky for Boston University Photography.

Top: JRS and sculptor Marc Mellon pose with Mellon's bust of JRS. Allan Dines Photography. *Bottom:* Neil Welliver's portrait of President John Silber, November 13, 1989. Pop was insulted when he first saw Neil's portrait, but my sisters and I have become fond of the scowling old man in the years since.
Photo by Kalman Zabarsky for Boston University Photography.

Top: This photograph gives some idea of the size of the Gala Celebration honoring John Silber in 2007. *Bottom:* Program for the Silber Gala Celebration.
Allan Dines Photography.

Top (left to right): Alan Leventhal, Peter Lynch, Rev. Charles Stith, Pres. Robert Brown, Fred Chicos, Beverly Brown, JRS, Loretta Cassidy, Gerry Cassidy, Bob Popeo, Tom Wolfe, Clare and Vartan Gregorian. Allan Dines Photography.
Bottom: Tom Wolfe and JRS converse before the Gala Celebration for John Silber in April 2007. Photo by Vernon Doucette for Boston University Photography.

Top: Barry Sloane, Suzanne Cutler, Barbara and Marshall Sloane, Dieuwke and Peter Fiedler. *Bottom:* Bill Adams and Don Perrin. Allan Dines Photography.

Top: Vita Paladino, director of the Howard Gotlieb Archival Research Center.
Bottom: President Robert Brown with President Emeritus John Silber.
Allan Dines Photography.

Top: JRS with Myra and Robert Kraft. *Bottom:* JRS with Patriots Equipment Manager sweatshirt, a gift from the Krafts. Allan Dines Photography.

Top, front row: Fred Chicos, Kevin White, Bob Popeo. *Background:* Ed King, Robert and Beverly Brown, JRS, unclear, and Gerry Cassidy. *Bottom:* William Weld (*left*) with Billy Bulger. Allan Dines Photography.

Top: Mayor Tom Menino spoke about the appropriateness of naming Sherborn Street, at the heart of Boston University, Silber Way. *Bottom:* Tom Menino with JRS. Allan Dines Photography.

Top: Clare Gregorian, Peter Lynch, and JRS. *Bottom:* JRS with Francis Stephens,
a longtime, popular chef at Boston University special events.
Allan Dines Photography.

Top: JRS and Rose Girouard enjoyed working together. Rose joined the dining service staff the same year John Silber became president of Boston University. *Bottom:* Rachel and Claudia Devlin. Claudia was very excited to be attending this great event, and I was proud to be one of the speakers. Allan Dines Photography.

Most of the family came to the Gala Celebration. Allan Dines Photography.

JRS addresses the crowded ballroom, flanked by his official portrait painted by Ray
Kinstler and the bust sculpted by Marc Mellon. Allan Dines Photography.

The grandchildren, after their Grandaddy's funeral, together at the Carlton Street house for the last time. Photo by Sonia Hathaway.

John Silber standing with his official Boston University portrait by Everett Raymond Kinstler, 1999.
Photo by Kalman Zabarsky for Boston University Photography.

Afterword

I HAVE RECENTLY BOUGHT A LITTLE HOUSE IN ROCKWALL, TEXAS, near Dallas, with the idea of spending winters there. How pleasant to be able to fly away from Boston and avoid the coldest months. The house is near a charming town center with some lovely old buildings, pleasing restaurants, and a few eclectic boutiques, and it offers a gratifying retreat from the ice-encrusted Northeast. My stepdaughter, Justine, lives in Rockwall with her husband, Terry, and my granddaughter, Kaitlyn. My son, John, lives nearby with his wife, Samantha, and two sons, Alistair and Dalton. And my youngest daughter, Claudia, has now relocated to the Dallas area as well.

My cousin Susanne, who inherited Grandmother Jewell's penchant for delivering veiled slights without ever straying from a well-mannered form, lives not far away in Fort Worth. When I told her I was writing this book she said, "Oh good, I'm sure that will be easier for you than trying to write a novel because you already know the story."

I look forward to rediscovering Texas. Most of Dallas is new territory for me so it will be fun scouting out new experiences with my children and grandchildren. And I can't wait to visit San Antonio to stroll along the Riverwalk and explore the Spanish missions once again. In Austin, I will drive out along the hill country roads to Lake Travis where once upon a time we sailed the *DRAMJACKYL*. I so enjoy hearing those genial Texan voices with their polite, old-fashioned manners.

Then, after a while, I will return to Boston and head to the North End for Pizza Primavera at Pizzeria Regina followed by gelato and espresso at Caffè Paradiso with my daughter, Mary Beth, and my son, James, and oldest grandson, Andrew. I would not want to miss the radiant turn of the leaves each autumn in New England, and I will renew my spirit and senses while immersing myself in the natural beauty of idyllic days at Squam Lake. An ideal balance.

Claudia with my grandkids: Kaitlyn, Andrew, Alistair, and Claudia holding Dalton. Rockwall, Texas.

Acknowledgements

John Silber, the man I knew so well, is pictured with such clarity and insight by Lance Morrow's quick, deft, and masterful brush-strokes. I'm glad I had finished writing the book before I asked Lance to write his foreword, or I might have read his work and thought there was not much I could add. Thank you, Lance.

I also want to thank Tom McCann for suggesting again and again that I write a book about my dad. I wasn't sure that I could even approach the subject, but he was convinced that I could, and should, do it.

I so enjoyed reminiscing with Christopher Ricks about my dad, and I thank him for reading my manuscript and for his pointed comments and expert advice.

A hearty thanks to Robin Stein, founder and leader of the Sequences writing group in Newton, Massachusetts. Thank you for reading the manuscript, making suggestions, and asking the questions that helped me tell the story I wanted to tell.

I greatly appreciate the help of Colin Riley, executive director of media relations, and Andrew Costello, photography manager at Boston University, who made it possible for me to search through their valuable inventory of photographs compiled over the many years by Boston University Photography. Thank you so much, Colin and Andy, for giving me a place to work, allowing me to look through the files I needed, and making the scans of photographs I wanted.

I am so grateful to Allan Dines who allowed me to use many of his photographs of Boston University events, and who also magically improved the quality of several older Silber family photos, sometimes making them clearly visible for the first time.

Thanks go to Deidre Randall and everyone at Peter E. Randall Publisher for their expertise and assistance every step of the way.

I am grateful for the help of my daughter, Mary Beth, the first to read my early chapters, who believed I had begun something worth pursuing, and to my stepdaughter, Justine, who read an early draft of the finished work and made many excellent fine points that improved the text greatly. Thanks go to my youngest daughter, Claudia, who helped often by allowing me to talk through several difficulties.

I appreciate the encouragement of my son, James, and grandson, Andrew, who also helped with the heavy boxes of old photographs so that I could choose what I needed for the book. I thank my older son, John, a movie blogger on his YouTube channel, the *Unwashed Critic*, for reading and remarking on the text and for remembering so much of our family history.

My greatest joy was in sharing this book with my sisters, Judith Ballan, Alexandra Mock, Martha Hathaway, Ruth Silber, and Caroline Lavender. Judith's close reading and insightful comments pointed me in the right direction several times. I feel lucky that Ruth captured the snapshot on the cover. It is so characteristic of Pop, grinning as he delighted in Ruth quickly snapping his picture while he was preparing to photograph her. And thank you, Caroline, for taking the picture of the trumpeting angels at the University of the Incarnate Word in San Antonio. Thank you Martha and Mike for reading and commenting on crucial passages and for remembering so much Boston University history. And I so appreciate Alexandra sharing essential memories. It was especially gratifying that all my sisters loved the book, and that the text prompted so many recollections from them that added depth to my narrative. Cheers to the Sister Hive!